Internet E and
Outlook Express 6
explained

Books Available

By the same authors:

If you would like to purchase a Companion Disc for any of our books listed above, **apart from this book and the ones marked with an asterisk**, containing the file/program listings which appear in them, then fill in the form at the back of the book and send it to Phil Oliver at the address given.

Internet Explorer 6 and Outlook Express 6 explained

by

P.R.M. Oliver
and
N. Kantaris

Bernard Babani (publishing) Ltd
The Grampians
Shepherds Bush Road
London W6 7NF
England

www.babanibooks.com

Please Note

Although every care has been taken with the production of this book to ensure that any projects, designs, modifications and/or programs, etc., contained herewith, operate in a correct and safe manner and also that any components specified are normally available in Great Britain, the Publishers and Author(s) do not accept responsibility in any way for the failure (including fault in design) of any project, design, modification or program to work correctly or to cause damage to any equipment that it may be connected to or used in conjunction with, or in respect of any other damage or injury that may be so caused, nor do the Publishers accept responsibility in any way for the failure to obtain specified components.

Notice is also given that if equipment that is still under warranty is modified in any way or used or connected with home-built equipment then that warranty may be void.

© 2002 BERNARD BABANI (publishing) LTD

First Published - May 2002

British Library Cataloguing in Publication Data:

A catalogue record for this book is available from the British Library

ISBN 0 85934 513 0

Cover Design by Gregor Arthur
Printed and Bound in Great Britain by Cox and Wyman Ltd

About this Book

Internet Explorer 6 and Outlook Express 6 explained has been written to help you get to grips with using the Internet and e-mail with the Microsoft software supplied with Windows XP.

These days you can't read a paper, listen to the radio, watch television very long, go shopping, or do your banking before you hear or see mention of the Internet. It has become an integral part of our lives over the last few years. What importance will it have after the next few years? If it follows the current trend and carries on growing exponentially, it could well become the most important technical development in the history of mankind. Everyone should test the water, but beware, the Web can be very habit forming!

An attempt has been made not to use too much 'jargon', but with this subject, some is inevitable, so a fairly detailed glossary of terms is included, which should be used with the text where necessary.

The book starts by overviewing the short history of the Internet (from the US military to rampant commercialism) and describes how the Web fits into the general scene.

A chapter follows explaining how you can obtain and install the software on your PC. How to go about connecting to the Internet and obtaining the technical help that may be needed is also very briefly covered. The book was written using version 6 of Internet Explorer and Outlook Express, working on a PC under the Windows XP operating system.

The following chapters describe this version of Internet Explorer and how best to use it for surfing the Web. Using Outlook Express 6 for handling your e-mail and your Newsgroup activities then follows.

Chapters are included on how to find your way around the Web using some of the many search 'engines' that are available, and how to recognise and guard against some of the unfortunate behaviour traits that have developed with the Internet.

One thing to remember when reading the book is that the whole Internet scenario is changing every day, especially the Web. What is there to look at today, may have gone, or changed shape, by tomorrow.

The book does not describe how to set up your PC, or how to use Windows. If you need to know more about the Windows environment, then we suggest you select an appropriate book from the 'Books Available' list - these are all published by BERNARD BABANI (publishing) Ltd.

Like the rest of our computer series, this book was written with the busy person in mind. It is not necessary to learn all there is to know about a subject, when reading a few selected pages can usually do the same thing quite adequately. Using this book, it is hoped that you will be able to come to terms with the Internet, Microsoft Explorer 6, Outlook Express 6 and the Web and get the most out of your computer in terms of efficiency, productivity and enjoyment, and that you will be able to do it in the shortest, most effective and informative way. Good luck.

About the Authors

Phil Oliver graduated in Mining Engineering at Camborne School of Mines and has specialised in most aspects of surface mining technology, with a particular emphasis on computer related techniques. He has worked in Guyana, Canada, several Middle Eastern and Central Asian countries, South Africa and the United Kingdom, on such diverse projects as: the planning and management of bauxite, iron, gold and coal mines; rock excavation contracting in the UK; international mining equipment sales and international mine consulting. Later he took up a lecturing position at Camborne School of Mines (part of Exeter University) in Surface Mining and Management. He has since retired from full-time lecturing to spend more time writing, consulting, and developing Web sites.

Noel Kantaris graduated in Electrical Engineering at Bristol University and after spending three years in the Electronics Industry in London, took up a Tutorship in Physics at the University of Queensland. Research interests in Ionospheric Physics, led to the degrees of M.E. in Electronics and Ph.D. in Physics. On return to the UK, he took up a Post-Doctoral Research Fellowship in Radio Physics at the University of Leicester, and then a lecturing position in Engineering at the Camborne School of Mines, Cornwall, (part of Exeter University), where he was also the CSM Computing Manager. At present he is IT Director of FFC Ltd.

Acknowledgements

We would like to thank both Microsoft for making this excellent software available free of charge, or commitment, on the Internet, and Future Publishing for supplying it on the CD ROMs that appear with their magazines PC Plus and .Net every month.

Trademarks

Arial and **Times New Roman** are registered trademarks of The Monotype Corporation plc.

HP and LaserJet are registered trademarks of Hewlett Packard Corporation.

IBM is a registered trademark of International Business Machines, Inc.

Intel is a registered trademark of Intel Corporation.

Microsoft, MS-DOS, Windows, Windows NT, Windows ME, Windows XP, and **Visual Basic**, are either registered trademarks or trademarks of Microsoft Corporation.

PostScript is a registered trademark of Adobe Systems Incorporated.

Macintosh, QuickTime and **TrueType** are registered trademarks of Apple Computer, Inc.

All other brand and product names used in the book are recognised as trademarks, or registered trademarks, of their respective companies.

Contents

1

The Internet

As you almost certainly know, if you have a computer and can connect to the Internet you can access millions of Web pages and use e-mail for keeping in touch with your friends, family and maybe more important for professional reasons.

There are several packages, most of them freely available now, that make this whole procedure very easy, once you know how. One of our favourites is Microsoft's Explorer 6 Web browser and Outlook Express 6 which comes with it. At the time of writing, this was becoming the most popular browser in use. If your PC has Windows XP, or later, you will already have it; if not, we will point you in the right direction, but first we must set the scene.

What is the Internet? - A Brief History

If you are not into 'history' then by all means skip this section. It's your book after all!

The universal use of Web sites and e-mail has become possible because of the explosive growth of the Internet in the last few years. So how did this all come about?

In the mid 1960s with the cold war very prominent, the US military faced a strange strategic problem. How could the country successfully communicate after a possible nuclear war? They would need a command and control communication network linking the cities, states and military bases, etc. But, no matter how the network was protected it would always be vulnerable to the impact of a nuclear attack and if the network had a control centre it would be the first to go.

As a solution, the concept was developed that the network itself should be assumed to be unreliable at all times and should be designed to overcome this unreliability. To achieve this, all the nodes (devices attached to the network, which have their own address and use the network as a means of communication) would be equal in status, each with its own authority to originate, pass, and receive messages. The messages themselves would be divided into small parts, or packets, with each being separately addressed. The transmission of each packet of data would begin at a specified source node, and end at another specified destination node, but would find its own way through the network, with the route taken being unimportant. With this concept, if sections of the network were destroyed, that wouldn't matter as the packets would use the surviving parts.

The National Physical Laboratory, here in the UK, set up the first test network on these principles in 1968. Shortly afterwards, the Pentagon's Advanced Research Projects Agency (ARPA) funded a larger, more ambitious project in the USA, with the high-speed 'supercomputers' of the day as the network nodes.

In 1969, the first such node was installed in UCLA. By December of that year, there were four nodes on the infant network, which was named ARPANET, after its sponsor. The four computers could transfer data on dedicated high-speed transmission lines, and could be programmed remotely from the other nodes. For the first time, scientists and researchers could share one another's computer facilities from a long distance. By 1972 there were thirty-seven nodes in ARPANET.

It soon became apparent, however, that much of the traffic on ARPANET was not long-distance computing, but consisted of news and personal messages. Researchers were using ARPANET not only to collaborate on projects and to exchange ideas on work, but to socialise. They had their own personal accounts on the ARPANET computers, and their own personal addresses for electronic mail and they were very enthusiastic about this particular new service, which we now know as e-mail.

Throughout the 70s, the ARPA network grew, its decentralised structure making expansion easy as it could accommodate different types of computers, as long as they could speak the standard packet-switching language. ARPA's original standard for communication was known as NCP short for 'Network Control Protocol', but this was soon superseded by the higher-level standard known as TCP/IP, which has survived until today.

TCP, or 'Transmission Control Protocol', converts messages into streams of packets at the source, then reassembles them back into messages at the destination. IP, or 'Internet Protocol', handles the addressing.

Over the years, ARPANET itself became a smaller and smaller part of the growing proliferation of other networked machines, but TCP/IP continued to link them all. As the 70s and 80s advanced, many different groups found themselves in possession of powerful computers. It was fairly easy to link these computers to the growing global network. As the use of TCP/IP, which was in the public domain by that time, became more common, entire other networks were incorporated into the **Internet**.

In 1984 the National Science Foundation became involved and created the new NSFNET linking newer and faster supercomputers with bigger and faster links. Other US government agencies joined the bandwagon, including NASA, the National Institutes of Health, and the Department of Energy.

ARPANET itself formally died in 1989, but its functions not only continued but were steadily improved. In Europe, major international 'backbone' networks started to provide connectivity to many millions of computers on a large number of other networks. Commercial network providers in both the US, Europe and Asia were beginning to offer Internet access and support on a competitive basis to any interested parties. In fact the extended use of the Internet cost the original founders little or nothing extra, since each new node was independent, and had to handle its own technical requirements and funding.

Now in the new century there are millions of nodes in the Internet, scattered throughout the world, with more coming on-line all the time and many more millions of people using this, often named 'Information Super Highway', every day.

Built to be indestructible and with no centralised control, it's no wonder the word 'anarchistic' is often bandied around when the Internet is discussed!

Why Use the Internet?

Now we know what the Internet is, what can we use it for? Basically, five things spring to mind; three are the reason for this book, and the others are mentioned briefly for completeness:

- Browsing, or surfing the Net.
- Sending and receiving e-mail messages.
- Taking part in News, or discussion groups.
- Accessing data stored on distant computers.
- Transferring data and program files from and to these distant computers.

Surfing the Net

The World Wide Web, or Web as we shall call it, consists of client computers (yours and mine) and server computers which handle multimedia documents with 'hypertext' links built into them. Clicking the links on a page in a Web browser on your PC, like Internet Explorer, brings documents located on a distant server to your screen, irrespective of the server's geographic location. Documents may contain text, images, sounds, movies, interactive programs (scripts), or a combination of these, in other words - multimedia.

Surfing the Web just means moving from site to site and following the links that catch your eye.

E-mail

Electronic mail, has to be one of the main uses of the Internet. It is very much faster that letter mail, which is known as 'snailmail' by regular e-mail users. It consists of electronic text, that is transmitted, sometimes in seconds, to anywhere else in the World that is connected to a main network. E-mail can also be used to send software and other types of files which are 'attached' to your message. As we shall see in later chapters, modern software such as Outlook Express makes this a very easy process.

Newsgroups

Discussion groups, or 'newsgroups', are another feature of the Internet that are easily accessed with Outlook Express. On the Internet they are generally known as USENET and consist of many, many thousands of separate groups which let you freely participate in discussions on a vast number of subjects.

Long Distance Computing

Using a program like Telnet you can maintain accounts on distant computers, run programs from them as if they were on your own PC, and generally make use of powerful supercomputers a continent away.

File Transfers

There is a fantastic amount of free software available over the Internet, as well as a multitude of text and graphics files on almost any subject you care to mention.

File transfers carried out with a protocol known as FTP, allow Internet users to access remote machines and retrieve these for their own use. This protocol is also used to upload files to a distant server when you build and maintain your own Web site.

The World Wide Web

Up until not many years ago all of these activities required very expensive computing facilities and a large measure of computer literacy. Times have changed, however, and it is now possible to very easily and cheaply install a modem in your PC, connect to the Internet and with a Web browser, like Microsoft's Internet Explorer 6, carry them out with very little technical knowledge. Hence the reason for this book, to help you on your way.

The World Wide Web, WWW, W3, or Web as we shall call it, was initially developed in Switzerland by CERN (the European Laboratory for Particle Physics), to form a distributed hypermedia system. It now consists of Web client computers (yours and mine) and server computers handling multimedia documents with hypertext links built into them. Client computers use browser software (like Internet Explorer) to view pages of these documents, one at a time. Server computers use Web server software to maintain the documents for us to access.

If you have used the Help pages of Windows you are familiar with a hypertext document. It contains links that you click with the mouse pointer to jump to other information. The advantage of hypertext in a Web document is that if you want more information about a particular subject, you just click on it and another page is opened for you to read or look at. In fact, documents can be linked to other documents (or graphics) by completely different authors and stored in completely different computers; much like footnoting, but you can get the referenced document instantly!

So, to access the Web, you run a browser program, in our case Microsoft Explorer 6, which reads files and documents, and fetches them from other sources on the Internet into the memory of your PC.

So Web browsers, like Explorer, provide users of computer networks with a consistent means to access a variety of media in a very simplified fashion. They have changed the way people view and create information, and have formed the first true global 'hypermedia' network. No wonder their use has taken off so dramatically in the last few years. There can't be many people around nowadays that don't use the Internet at all.

Hypermedia is a superset of hypertext - it is any medium with pointers to other media. This means that the latest browsers display formatted text, images, play sound clips, or video type animations. Some of these, however, may require extra hardware, like a sound card, in your computer.

HTML - The Original Web Language

You may never get involved with this, but most Web documents are still created by authors using a language called HTML (HyperText Markup Language). This offers short codes, or tags, to designate graphical elements and hypertext links. Clicking a link on a Web page in your browser, brings documents located on a distant server to your screen, irrespective of the server's geographic location. Documents may contain text, images, sounds, movies, or a combination of these, in other words - multimedia.

How Links are Named

Every link in a hypertext Web document has to have a unique address and for you to use your browser properly you should understand these addresses, or Uniform Resource Locators, (URLs for short). It is possible to represent nearly any file or service on the Internet with a URL and several examples are given on the next page.

The first part of the URL (before the two slashes) specifies the method of access, as described on the next page. The second is typically the domain name of the computer on which the data, or service, is located. Further parts may specify the names of folders and files, the port to connect to, or the text to search for in a database. A URL is always a single unbroken line with **no spaces**.

Here are some examples of URLs:

http://www.ex.ac.uk/location/book.html

This would connect to an HTTP server (in this case a Web server at the University of Exeter) and would retrieve an HTML file (a Web file).

ftp://www.xerox.com/pub/file.txt

This would open an FTP connection to www.xerox.com and retrieve a text file.

news:alt.sex

This would read the latest Usenet news by connecting to a specified news host and would return the articles in the alt.sex newsgroup in hypermedia format.

The first part of the URL (before the two slashes) gives the method of access at that address, as follows:

- **http** - a hypertext document or directory.
- **Gopher** - a gopher document or menu.
- **ftp** - a file or folder available for downloading.
- **news** - a newsgroup.
- **Telnet -** a computer system that you can log into from across the Internet.
- **WAIS** - a database or document on a WAIS (**W**ide **A**rea **I**nformation **S**earch) database.
- **file** - a file located on a local drive.

Sites that run Web servers are typically named with a www. at the beginning of the network address. As we shall see, Microsoft Explorer allows you to specify a URL and thus connect to that document, or service. When selecting hypertext links in a Web page, you are actually sending a request to open a URL. In this way, hyperlinks can be made not only to other texts and media, but also to other network services. Web browsers are not simply Web clients, but are also full FTP, Gopher, and Telnet clients in their own rights.

All of these features are now easily available over ordinary phone lines, once you get direct Internet access through a local Internet Service Provider (ISP), as explained in the next chapter.

2

Internet Exploring

At the time of writing this book, the Web browser market arguably only has one main player, Microsoft. To establish its dominant position in the market, Microsoft, as well as providing good products, has given away all its browser products and has included Explorer as part of most of its Windows, Office and Works packages.

Not so many years ago Netscape had the browser market to itself, but they could not survive Microsoft's power and tactics without being taken over, and they now form part of the AOL empire.

Microsoft have made a habit of dominating their markets. Look at DOS, Windows and then the applications like Excel and Word, etc. The Web browser market went the same way. At the time of writing 80 - 95% of the people who visit our Web sites now use a version of Explorer. That really says it all.

Windows Versions

Internet Explorer 6 comes with Microsoft Windows XP as standard, but you can also use it with the following earlier versions of Windows: Windows 98, Windows NT 4.0 with Service Pack SP6a and higher, Windows 2000 and Windows Me.

If you are using Windows 95 or an earlier version, you will have to upgrade your system to use Explorer 6 and Outlook Express 6.

What's New with Version 6

Web Privacy Tools - protect your privacy and allow you to control the personal information Web sites collect about you.

Fault Collection - you can extract information about an Explorer problem and upload it to Microsoft for analysis.

Image Toolbar - allows you to quickly and easily save, e-mail, or print pictures from your Web page, as well as view all your saved pictures in the My Pictures folder.

Media Bar - provides a user interface for locating and playing media such as music, video, or mixed-media files within the browser window. You can control the audio volume, choose which media files or tracks to play, and access different media on the Microsoft **WindowsMedia.com** Web site or on your own computer.

Auto Image Resize - If pictures are too large to display in the browser window, the new automatic picture resizing feature resizes the pictures so they fit within the dimensions of the browser window.

Updated Browser Look - When used with Windows XP you get new stylized buttons in the browser toolbar, more colourful menu background and toolbar areas.

Java applets - only run in Internet Explorer 6 after the Java VM is installed. This is done on demand when a user first encounters a page that uses a Java Applet.

Development Features - Explore 6 contains many new 'rich Web-based Application features' which are outside the scope of this book.

Outlook Express 6.0 - includes new security features that can help protect your computer from harmful e-mail and blocks potentially harmful attachments.

Computer Hardware

First, you obviously need a computer! We have written this book with the current most common new combination - a PC running under Windows XP.

If you buy a new PC, it will probably come with all the software we are concerned with here already installed. In this case you have no problems. Otherwise, the minimum hardware requirements to run Explorer 6 and Outlook Express 6, are a 486 DX/66 MHz, or higher, PC with 16 MB of RAM for Windows 98, 32 MB of RAM minimum for Windows NT/2000/Me.

To install the browser alone requires up to 13 MB of hard disc space, depending on your version of Windows. As the installation is actually an upgrading of your version of Windows, most of this disc space must be available on the disc drive that holds the Windows system itself.

Ideally you will need the fastest Pentium PC with as much RAM and hard disc space as you can get your hands on!

You also need a connection to the Internet, via a Modem, Ethernet Card, or ISDN direct digital phone line. A digital ISDN line is faster than a modem connection, but is considerably more expensive, at the moment.

Getting Online

Unless you are lucky enough to have a PC which is connected to a Local Area Network (LAN) which has Internet access, you will need a modem to be able to communicate with the rest of the world. This is a device that converts data so that it can be transmitted over the telephone system.

You will also need to find, and possibly subscribe to, a suitable Internet Service Provider. There are many such providers in the UK. Most can be listed on the Web by accessing the following address:

http://thelist.internet.com/

When last we did this it opened the Web page shown below in Fig. 2.1.

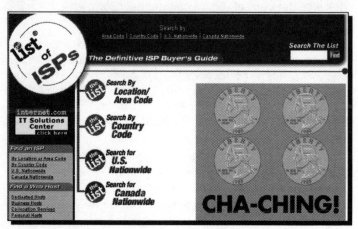

Fig. 2.1 Getting a List of Internet Service Providers

Clicking a 'Country Code' link and looking under the UK, or wherever else you are based, opens a very extensive listing of the ISPs available.

Another way would be to buy an Internet based PC magazine from your local newsagent and look at the reviews and adverts. Also you could try your friendly neighbourhood computer store, the telephone directory, or possibly adverts in the computer section of your local paper.

There are providers who give free Internet access and pay for the service with advertising or from telephone line revenues. But as in most walks of life, you get what you pay for.

Be careful before committing yourself to one provider as the quality of service can vary considerably. One thing we can't do here is make specific recommendations, but try and find someone who uses the company you decide on, or have a trial period with them.

What you are ideally looking for is **full dial-up SLIP or PPP connection with unlimited WWW access to the Internet**, and this should be possible by dialling a local number to your provider's access point. (SLIP and PPP are only two communication standards that you need to have, but do not need to understand).

The local call access will mean your phone bills should not be excessive, especially if you do your Internet accessing in off-peak times. The unlimited access means you will not pay any extra to your Internet Provider no matter how many hours you spend on line, just your monthly fee, if any.

Many ISPs now provide an 'all in' service, where you pay them a set monthly fee to cover all your internet access, with no extra phone charges. This can cost in the region of £15 per month, but there is a lot of competition.

From now on in this book, we assume that you have an active connection to the Internet. Trouble-shooting this is not within our remit!

Getting your Software

If you already have your version of Explorer 6 and Outlook Express 6 up and running on your computer you can skip the rest of this section. If not, you may want to obtain the software. When you are actually connected to the Internet you can download Microsoft's Internet Explorer software absolutely free by clicking this button on their Web site at:

www.microsoft.com/uk/windows/

If you are not yet connected, you obviously can't do this, but there is a another way. Some computer magazines that come with CD-ROMs carry Web browsers on them. Our favourites are *PC Plus* and *.net*, which most months include the latest browsers from both Netscape and Microsoft.

With the size of this browser this can save many hours of valuable time downloading. The saving in your phone bill may well pay for the magazine as well.

Installing Internet Explorer

If you download the program, you are prompted to download a 500 KB setup file called ie6setup.exe. We suggest you

save this in a suitable folder on your hard disc. Then simply double-clicking the downloaded **ie6setup** icon, as shown here, will start the installation procedure whenever you are ready. During the setup, you can choose the type of installation you prefer, and Internet Explorer will download only the files you need.

From the CD-ROM just follow the instructions and click **Next** to continue. With either method, once you have accepted the licence agreement, the procedure will start with a window similar to ours shown in Fig. 2.2 below. If you do not have enough space on your hard disc, you will be told to free up more room and try again. Good luck.

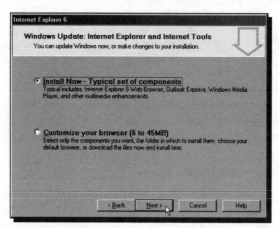

Fig. 2.2 Getting Under way with the Installation Procedure

If you want to abort the procedure at any time press the **Cancel** button, but be warned on no account should you then switch off your PC until your old setup is returned. A few minutes of nail biting, hoping there will not be a power cut! The procedure seems to work well, in fact the next time you start the installation procedure it even gives you the option of carrying on from where you last aborted. We accepted this option without any problems.

When you regain control of your PC, you may well find your desktop has a new Explorer icon added to the Quick Launch bar, (to the right of the *start* button) as shown here in Fig. 2.3.

Here two Explorer icons can be seen, one at the top of the *start* Menu itself, and one below on the Quick Launch bar. Clicking either of these will launch the program, as we shall see next. An Outlook Express entry should also appear on the *start* Menu as shown.

Fig. 2.3 The Windows XP Start Menu

To remove an entry from the top section of the *start* menu, such as the one for Explorer, right-click on it and select the **Remove from This List** menu option. You will still be able to open Internet Explorer from the Quick Launch bar, but you will make more space on the *start* menu for other often used programs.

Starting Internet Explorer

Clicking either of the Internet Explorer icons shown in Fig 2.3 will open the browser. The first time you do this it will probably start the New Connection Wizard, which steps you through the process of establishing your link to the Internet.

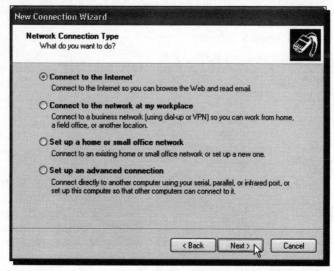

Fig. 2.4 The New Connection Wizard

This Wizard can make the process of setting up your Internet connection quite painless. You can open it at any time with the **Tools**, **Internet Options** menu command by clicking the **Setup** button on the **Connections** tabbed sheet. Obviously how you complete the options that are offered will depend on your particular system and circumstances.

Before starting this operation be sure to find out from your system administrator or your Internet Service Provider exactly what settings you will need to enter.

After all this you get your first look at the new browser. If all is well and your Internet connection is open, you may get an opening screen which may look something like that shown in Fig. 2.5. What actually appears will depend on Microsoft, or your ISP, and will also change very often.

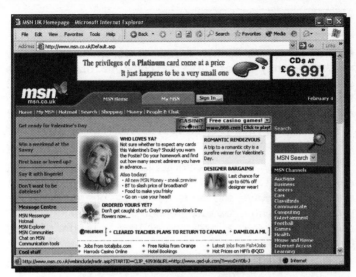

Fig. 2.5 A Typical First Opening Screen

Note that when the Explorer is actually downloading data from the network, the Status Indicator on the right of the menu bar, and shown here, gives an active display and the status bar gives an indication of what is actually happening.

The default opening screen shown in Fig. 2.5 is that of **msn.co.uk**, a portal service provided by Microsoft. They would rather you spent all your time working in their territory!

You can control what Web page, called your home page, is displayed when you start Explorer, in the **General** settings sheet opened with the **Tools**, **Internet Options** menu command. Select **Use Current** to make any currently open page your home page, or **Use Blank** to show a clear window whenever you start up Explorer. The **Use Default** option lets you start up in **msn.co.uk** again.

Your PC Settings

Before we go any further, a few words on screen display resolutions may be useful. Your computer may well have started life set to a screen resolution of 800 x 600 pixels. It then displays a screen of 800 pixels wide and 600 pixels high on the monitor. The bigger the monitor you have, the bigger the screen resolution you can use, as everything gets smaller as the resolution goes up.

For Web browsing you want as large a resolution as you can get so that you can fit more on the screen. Web pages are almost always too large to fit on one screen. We recommend using a resolution of 800 x 600 if you have a 14" or 15" monitor, and a resolution of 1024 x 768 for 17" and larger monitors.

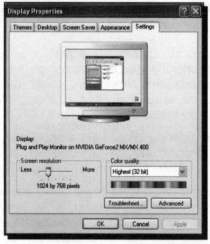

Fig. 2.6 Controlling your Screen Resolution

It is easy to change the screen settings, but Windows may have to be re-started for them to take effect. Click the **Start**, button, and open the **Control Panel,** double-click on the **Display** icon, and then click the Settings tab to open the window shown in Fig. 2.6 above. Another way to open this box is to right-click on the Desktop and select **Properties** from the opened menu. The details shown were for one of our PCs, yours will almost certainly be different. Both the **Color quality** setting and the **Screen resolution** slider are interlinked. The higher the colour setting the lower will be the maximum Desktop area, or resolution. In our case above with a Highest Colour (32-bit) setting our maximum resolution was 1280 by 1024. With our overstressed eyes though we are not comfortable working with that resolution!

With this colour setting, you get near photographic image quality, and graphics, or pictures, look much better than with only a 256 colour setting. You will find the Web much more entertaining if you surf with thousands, or millions, of colours, instead of just 256.

A Trial Run

You should now be up and running with the Internet Explorer 6, so let's do something. There are many millions of Web pages to look at, so where do we start? You may have started already from the opening page, but there is one UK institution that we all know and love, the Government! They have spent time and money on their Web presentations, so let's take a quick look.

 Start Explorer, if it is not already going, log onto the Internet, and click the **Search** button, shown here, which is on the button bar known as the Toolbar. Click on **New**, which opens the Search panel on the left of the Explorer window, which should be similar to that shown here in Fig. 2.7.

We will discuss Web searches again in a later chapter, so for now type 'UK government' in the text box, and click the **Search** button to 'Start Searching' as we did here.

Fig. 2.7 The Search Bar

In our case, this opened a 'UK Plus' search page in the panel, and searched for references to the 'UK government', as shown in Fig. 2.8 below. Explorer uses different search engines so your search may not use UK Plus, but another one. Hopefully the results will be similar!

Fig. 2.8 Using the Search Bar

UK Plus is just one of the many search utilities, or 'engines' available for finding your way round the Web. It found several relevant Web pages, and brought details of what it considered to be the most relevant ones to the search pane on the left. Search tools are very powerful and useful facilities, which we shall discuss further in a later chapter.

In our case the third entry above will do. Clicking the underlined Home Office link opens the page we were looking for, as shown on the right in Fig. 2.8 above.

Move the mouse pointer over the menu bar (on the left side of the Home Office page) and when it changes to a 'hand' over the **Passports** item, as shown above, click the mouse button. This will open a page pointing you to the UK Passport Agency's own Web site, shown next in Fig. 2.9.

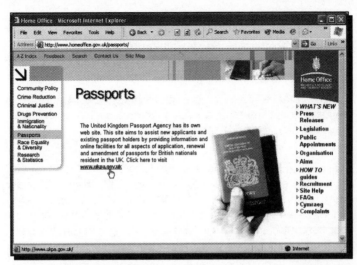

Fig. 2.9 Following Links Between Web Pages

Clicking the link, as shown above, will take you to the main Passports site. If you need a new passport, or want information on renewing one, this is a very useful site. That's the beauty of the Internet, once you find your way around you can get almost any up to date information you need without moving from your desk.

If we had known the URL address of the site we wanted, **www.ukpa.gov.uk** in our case, we could have typed it straight into the Explorer **Address** bar, as shown below.

Fig. 2.10 Using the Address Bar

This will open the Web page when the Enter key on the keyboard is pressed, or the **Go** button (on the right of the bar) is clicked.

Again try moving the mouse pointer around the screen. When it passes over some of the screen items it changes to a hand, as shown in our illustrations. What that means is that each of these graphics is actually a link to another Web page. The status bar, at the bottom of the screen, shows the URL address of the link pointed to, and the banner that opens next to the pointer describes the function of the link. Clicking any of these links on the page will open another page, which may well contain more links.

We will leave it to you to explore these sites further. You may find some interesting information, or on the other hand, they may help to send you to sleep.

NOTE - If a Web page is taking a long time to load you can open another browser window with the **File**, **New**, **Window** menu command, or the <Ctrl+N> keystroke shortcut. You can have as many Web pages open at the same time as your computer's memory will hold, all doing different things.

Be warned though, eventually you will cause a memory overflow and Explorer will lock up. This always seems to happen at the worst possible moment and the only solution is to use the dreaded <Ctrl+Alt+Delete> key combination and shut down the offending program. Sometimes it is even better to re-boot your computer, as this clears all the temporary 'junk' files and settings and lets you start with a clean slate.

3

Basic Program Features

Explorer Screen Layout

The illustration below shows an Explorer 6 window with the three main Toolbars and the new Media bar showing.

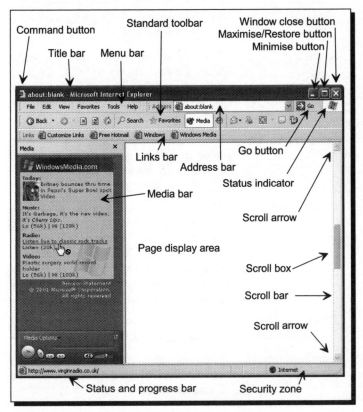

Fig. 3.1 The Main Explorer Features

It is perhaps worth spending some time looking at the various parts that make up this window, which is subdivided into several areas with the following functions:

Area	*Function*
Command button	Clicking on this program icon button, located in the upper-left corner of each window, displays the pull-down Control menu which can be used to control the window. It includes commands for restoring, maximising, minimising, moving, sizing, and closing the window.
Title bar	The bar which displays the title of the current Web page.
Menu bar	The bar which allows you to choose from several menu options. Clicking on a menu item displays the pull-down menu associated with that item.
Minimise button	The button you point to and click to reduce an application to an icon on the Windows Taskbar at the bottom of the screen.
Restore button	The button you point to and click to restore the window to its former size. When that happens, the Restore button changes to a Maximise button which is used to fill the screen with the active window.
Close button	The red X button that you click to close the window.
Standard toolbar	A bar of icons that you click to carry out some of the more common Explorer actions.

Address bar	Shows the location of the current page, or the URL of the new page to go to next.
Links bar	Links which automatically load on-line Web pages and can be set up with your own favourites.
Media bar	A user interface for locating and playing media such as music, video, or mixed-media files.
Status indicator	Activates when data transfer is taking place.
Page display	The main body of the window that displays Web pages.
Explorer bars	Vertical bars in the left side of the browser window that open when the Search, Favorites, Media and History Toolbar buttons are actioned.
Scroll bars	If the contents of a window will not fit in it, scroll bars are added to the right and/or the bottom of the window.
Scroll arrows	The arrowheads at each end of a scroll bar which you can click to scroll the screen up and down, or left and right.
Scroll box	Dragging this box up or down the scroll bar will rapidly scroll through a Web page.
Status bar	The animated bar that shows the progress of a downloading operation, the address of the link or graphic, pointed to by the mouse, and other status messages.
Security zone	Shows the security settings for the Web site being accessed.

As is now becoming a standard feature with Microsoft programs, at first glance an empty Explorer window can look a little grey and lifeless, but when you move the mouse pointer over the toolbar its buttons 'light up' when they are active. This is a very pleasing feature, the window being designed not to detract from the Web pages being viewed in it.

Menu Bar Options

Each option on the menu bar has associated with it a pull-down sub-menu. This follows the normal Windows convention, so to access the menu, either click the mouse on an option, or press the <Alt> key, which causes the first option of the menu (in this case **File**) to be highlighted, then use the arrow keys to highlight any of the options in the menu. Pressing either the <Enter> key, or the left mouse button, reveals the pull-down sub-menu of the highlighted menu option. The sub-menu of the **File** option is shown here.

Fig. 3.2 The File Sub-menu

Menu options can also be activated directly by pressing the <Alt> key followed by the underlined letter of the required option. With this version of the program, the underlining only shows after the <Alt> key has been used. Thus pressing <Alt+F>, opens the **File** sub-menu shown in Fig. 3.2 above.

You can use the up and down arrow keys to move the highlighted bar up and down a sub-menu, or the right and left arrow keys to move along the options in the Menu bar. Pressing the <Enter> key selects the highlighted option or executes the highlighted command. Pressing the <Esc> key once, closes the pull-down sub-menu, while pressing the <Esc> key for a second time, closes the Menu system.

Note that those commands which are not available at any specific time will be inactive and appear on the menu in a lighter colour. In our example on the previous page the options **E**d**it** and **S**ave are not available.

Keyboard Shortcuts

Some of the menu options have keyboard shortcuts attached to them. These are very useful to people who are more used to the keyboard than the mouse. In the **File** sub-menu there are several. For example, pressing <Ctrl+N>, the 'N' key with the 'Ctrl' key also depressed, will open a new browser window.

We have listed the available shortcuts in Appendix A.

Mouse Right-click Menu

You can use your right mouse button to click objects on a page and see a drop-down shortcut, or context, menu with contents that depend on what you click:

On a link	The menu items refer to the page specified by the link.
On an image	They refer to the image file specified by the image.
On background	They apply to the current page, its text, or its background image.
On the Title bar	They allow you to control the current window.

On the Toolbar	The menu items help you customise the Toolbar area.
On a Scroll bar	They give you options to scroll to different parts of the current page.

This example shows the options that were available when the mouse was right-clicked on the picture.

Fig. 3.3 A Right-click Context Menu

The actions available were: Opening the page linked to the image in the current window, or in a new one, saving the linked page to a file on disc, or sending it to the printer; saving the picture to a file on disc, setting it as the Windows wallpaper or an item on the Windows desktop; copying the image or its URL to the clipboard; and adding the linked file to the Favorites list. Clicking on **Pr̲operties** would show details of the image file.

As usual, unavailable options are shown in grey.

The Standard Toolbar

Most Windows applications are now fully equipped with a Toolbar option, and Internet Explorer is no exception. It contains a series of buttons that you can click with your mouse pointer to quickly carry out a program function.

Fig. 3.4 The Default Standard Toolbar

Most of the buttons are pretty self-explanatory and have the following functions:

Button	*Function*
Back	Displays the previous page viewed, or selects from the drop-down history list.
Forward	Displays the next page on the history list.
Stop	Halts any on-line transfer of page data.
Refresh	Brings a fresh copy of the current Web page to the viewer.
Home	Displays your specified home page, with a Microsoft page as the default.
Search	Opens the Search bar with access to Microsoft selected search facilities.
Favorites	Opens the Favorites bar with access to your saved favourite sites, or bookmarks.
Media	Opens the Media bar which can locate and control the playing of music and videos.
History	Opens the History bar and displays a hierarchical list of the Web pages you have previously viewed. You can browse through these again in Offline mode.
Mail	Gives quick access to your e-mail and Newsgroup facilities.

Print   Prints the open Web page, or frame, using the current print settings.

Edit   Opens the current Web page in one of the available HTML editors on your system.

Discuss   Gives you access to discussion groups, or opens a wizard for you to set one up.

If the Toolbar is not showing when a window is opened, you simply open the **View** menu, select the **Toolbars** option and choose what features you want to show. This places a tick '√' character on the selected options. Selecting them again in the future, will toggle the options off.

Customising the Toolbar

You can customise your Toolbar from the dialogue box shown in Fig. 3.5 below which opens when you right-click on an empty section of the bar and select **Customize**.

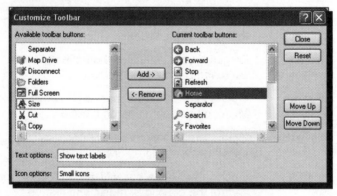

Fig. 3.5 The Customize Toolbar Dialogue Box

The pane in the left of this box shows that there are in fact eleven other Toolbar buttons available, as follows:

Map Drive   Opens a Wizard that lets you easily connect to a shared network folder. It also lets you assign a drive letter to it.

Disconnect Disconnects a shared network drive.

Folders Opens a Folders bar on the left of the Explorer window, so that you can easily access files on your computer.

Full Screen Sets the browser to display a full screen view but leaving a customisable Toolbar for viewing control. This is a superb feature.

Size Gives a choice of 5 font sizes for the browser to use.

Cut Cuts the current selection to the clipboard.

Copy Copies the current selection to the clipboard.

Paste Pastes the clipboard contents.

Encoding Lets you change the way the browser decodes Web pages from other countries.

Related Opens the Search bar to find Web pages with a similar content to the one you are currently viewing.

We also have a **Researcher** button for our Explorer Toolbar, which allows us to copy text and pictures from the active Web page to an Encarta Project. We assume you only get this when you have the Microsoft Encarta encyclopedia installed on your PC.

To add any of these other buttons to the Toolbar, simply select them in the **Available toolbar buttons** list and click the central **Add** button. To remove unwanted buttons from the bar you do the reverse and select them in the **Current toolbar buttons** list and then click on **Remove**. At any time, you can click the **Reset** button to return to the default Toolbar configuration.

If, like us, you find the Toolbar buttons a little on the large side you can change the way they appear on your screen. You have three choices in the **Text options** drop-down list, and once you are used to the program, selecting the **No text**

labels option removes the text completely and brings the icons much closer together.

We go one step further by selecting **Small icons** in the **Icon options** drop-down list. It is worthwhile experimenting with the settings here to find out which way you prefer your browser to operate.

Fig. 3.6 Button Options

Our example here in Fig. 3.6 shows the difference in the size of icons after these operations have been carried out. The 'before' and 'after' sections of the Toolbar are both displayed at the same scale.

With Explorer 6, you can also alter the layout of the Control bars by dragging them up or down with the mouse, as shown in the sequence below. The control area shrinks as you drag the frame up and expands again when it is dragged down.

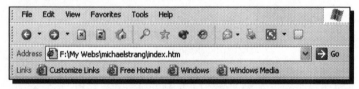

Fig. 3.7 Layout with Controls 'Maximised'

You can also try different combinations of controls in the same bars by dragging the vertical embossed lines between them. We show below our favourite arrangement of the control area, which includes all the important features, but takes up the minimum of screen space.

Fig. 3.8 A Good Working Layout for the Control Area

When you are happy with the layout and contents of the Toolbars we suggest you right-click on an empty section of the bar and select the **Lock the Toolbars** option.

The Address Bar

The **Address** bar is the main way of opening new Web pages. If you know the URL address of the page you want to look at, you can type it into this field. Then simply clicking the **Go** button, or pressing the <Enter> key will load the page, as long as you are connected to the Internet. If you are not, it will start the connection procedure. A pull-down menu, opened by clicking the down-arrow at the right of the field, lets you choose from the most recent locations you have typed here, which can save both effort and errors!

Fig. 3.9 Autocomplete Working in the Address Bar

The address bar also uses 'Autocomplete', a very useful feature which saves previous entries made for Web addresses, forms, and passwords. As you start to type a URL into the address bar, Explorer drops down a list of possible matches, as shown in Fig. 3.9 above. As you can see, you don't need to type the http://www part of the address, this is added automatically later. If you have previously visited the site, you get a scrolling list of all the matching pages visited. You pick the one you want from the list, or just keep typing if the address you want is not shown.

To delete entries from the Address bar, you must clear your History folder. On the **Tools** menu click **Internet Options** and on the **General** tab click the **Clear History** button. You should not do this, of course, if you want to return offline to any of the Web pages that have been stored there. You cannot clear individual entries from the list of saved entries without editing the Windows Registry, which we do not recommend unless you really know what you are doing.

The address bar also automatically corrects common mistakes made in the 'http://' and 'ftp://' part of an address. Mind you if you don't type them in, you won't make too many mistakes here!

You can also carry out an 'Auto-Search' from the address bar, by typing '?', 'Find' or 'Go' and then the words you want to search for. When you press the Return key the search will be performed. You can turn off this feature, and adjust some of the other search features in the **Advanced** tab sheet of the **Tools**, **Internet Options** dialogue box, as shown below.

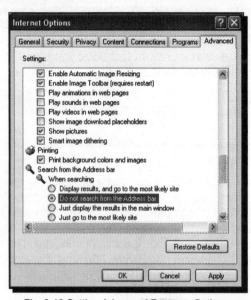

Fig. 3.10 Setting Advanced Program Options

While this box is open it is worth seeing what control you do have over the browser settings. In our example above, for example, we have 'turned off' the options to play animations, sounds and videos. This was done by simply clicking in the square box to the left of each item. Clicking again will turn the option back on and place a tick in the box.

Turning off the above options will considerably speed up the loading of many Web pages. You could even go one step further and de-select the **Show pictures** option. This will turbo-charge the browser, but make the Web a little boring, unless, of course, it is only the text you are interested in.

The Links Bar

As we saw earlier in the chapter, by default, under the Address bar there is a set of Links buttons which open various online pages prepared for you by Microsoft, or the Internet Service Provider who supplied your browser. These links are well worth exploring and may give you some ideas about where to go on the Web, and indeed, what can be usefully achieved instead of just surfing aimlessly from one link to another.

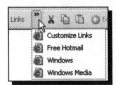

Fig. 3.11 Links Bar

To make more room for viewing Web pages we usually turn off this feature, but a useful trick is to drag the Links bar to the left of another bar and shrink it so that all the link buttons disappear. You can then click the right double-arrow button to open a menu with all the links of the bar available, as shown here.

The Links buttons do not have to stay pointing to their preset pages as shown here. You can easily set them to hold your own most used sites, as described in the next chapter.

The Image Toolbar

A new and, we think, somewhat unnecessary feature of Explorer 6 is the Image Toolbar that opens whenever your mouse pointer 'hovers' over a Web page graphic larger than 130 x 130 pixels.

This bar, as shown here, has four buttons, which let you quickly save the image to disc, print it, e-mail it, or open the My Pictures folder. All very useful, but the right-click menu lets you do all these already, without the inconvenience of having a bar blocking off part of the picture.

We must admit that we have unceremoniously turned this feature off with the **Tools**, **Internet Options**, **Advanced**, **Enable Image Toolbar** toggle option (in the Multimedia section of the list).

Image Resizing

Also new to Explorer 6 is the Image Resize feature. This is switched on by default, and reduces the size of a large page graphic to fit in the Explorer window. In fact images will resize automatically as you change the size of the Explorer window.

Fig. 3.12 Image Resizing in Operation

Fig. 3.12 shows how this feature works. In the upper box the Explorer window is much too small for the image, so the picture is shrunk to fit. When the mouse pointer is moved onto the image the **Expand to regular size** button is displayed. If you click this the picture is then shown full size, as shown in the lower box. Of course only part of the image can then be displayed. Now when the mouse pointer is moved onto the image the **Fit image to window** button is opened. Clicking this will reverse the procedure.

This is quite a feature, as the image resolution and clarity is fairly well retained. If you don't like it you can switch it off, as before, with the **Tools**, **Internet Options**, **Advanced**, **Enable Automatic Image Resizing** toggle option (in the Multimedia section of the list).

Full Screen View

A feature of Explorer 6 is the option to browse using a full screen view. We often view the Web with several windows open at the same time, and so that we can see them all, they obviously have to be reduced in size. When you want to look at one page in more detail, clicking the **Full Screen** icon on the Toolbar, or pressing the **F11** key, shows it using the whole screen, except for a thin Toolbar along the top edge, and reduced scroll bars if necessary. Even the Toolbar can be customised by right-clicking it. With the screen resolution we use, we can get the Toolbar icons, the Menu bar and the Address bar onto the Full Screen Toolbar. We usually have **Auto Hide** selected as well, so that the Toolbar itself only displays when you move the pointer over it.

The rest of the time the Web page is displayed with no Windows 'clutter' at all, as in our example in Fig. 3.13 on the next page.

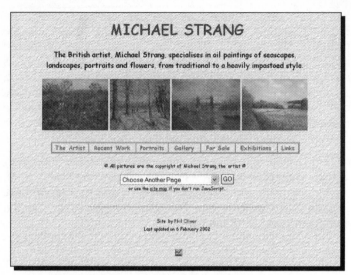

Fig. 3.13 One of Our Web Pages Viewed Fullscreen

This option really makes viewing Web pages a pleasure. Clicking the **Full Screen** icon, or pressing **F11**, again returns you to the window layout you had before.

General Option Settings

Like most Windows programs, you control the other ways Internet Explorer operates for you, by changing settings in a series of tabbed sheets accessed with the **Tools**, **Internet Options** menu command, as we saw earlier. Perhaps we should now look at some of the other options available here.

In the General tab sheet, shown open on the next page, you can control which page is loaded when you start Explorer, or click the Home icon. We are sure you will not want the Microsoft default **Home page** option, so we suggest you load the page you do want before you open this dialogue box and then select the **Use Current** option.

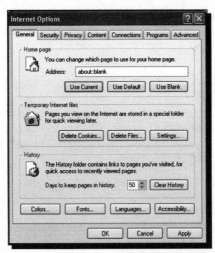

Fig. 3.14 The General Internet Options Sheet

The **Temporary Internet files** options let you control the hard disc cache where the program stores all the files it downloads. The **History** section gives you some control over the details of the pages you have recently visited which are displayed when you click the **History** Toolbar icon. If you ever run short of hard disc space, clearing these two options will release that space being used for temporary file storage.

The **Fonts** and **Languages** buttons let you set the default fonts and language used by your browser, and the **Accessibility** button lets you override any font size, colour or type settings made in a Web page. This is not usually a good thing to do, unless you have very strong preferences, as Web page authors usually spend a lot of time specifying their page settings to get the visual effects they want.

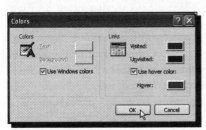

The **Colors** button gives you control of the colours in a Web page. We suggest you leave the **Use Windows colors** option selected,

Fig. 3.15 Controlling Colour

but select **Use hover color** as shown in Fig. 3.15. With 'hover' colour set, as shown, the links on a Web page change colour to a bright red whenever you pass the pointer over them.

While you are at it, take a good look around the other options on the other tabbed sheets. If an option is not self explanatory, you can click the help button shown here [?] (which is located in the top right of the window), then click the 'What's this' pointer on the offending item to get more details of its function, as shown below.

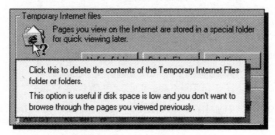

Fig. 3.16 Using 'What's this' Help

Saving Pictures

For many people, one of the big attractions of the Internet is the enormous collection of photographs and other graphical data that is freely available. Whatever your preferences, all you have to do is search until you find them.

But how can I download a picture onto my PC and have it to look at, whenever I want? I hear you asking.

If you have followed this chapter up to this point you will not need to ask, you will probably be doing it already. If not, the procedure is very easy. Once you have found the picture you want on a Web page, simply right-click your mouse on it and select from the object menu that opens.

Our example in Fig. 3.17 on the next page shows a photograph of a consultant surveying from one of our Web sites, with the right-click menu options that are available.

Fig. 3.17 Using the Right-click Menu to Save a Picture

Clicking on **Save Picture As...** will open the Save As dialogue box for you to enter the **File name** and folder to **Save in** details. When you have done this, simply click the **Save** button to capture your picture. Don't fill up your hard disc though!

Explorer Help

The trend these days is for programs to be shipped with very little in the way of a manual and a much less detailed built-in Help system than was the norm a few years ago. We shouldn't really complain about this as maybe that is why you are reading this book!

Internet Explorer 6 has a built-in Help system, which is accessed with the **Help**, **Contents and Index** menu command. This opens a Windows XP type Help window, as shown in Fig. 3.18.

We strongly recommend that you work your way through all the listed items. Clicking on a closed book icon will open it and display a listing of its contents. Double-clicking on a list item will open a window with a few lines of Help information on the topic.

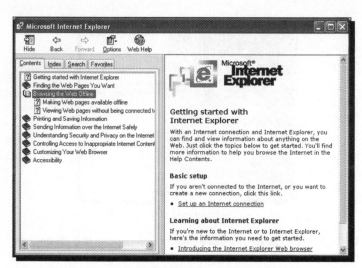

Fig. 3.18 Using Help with Internet Explorer

Another way of browsing the Help system is to click the **Index** tab and work your way through the alphabetic listing. The **Favorites** tab opens a page that lets you store help screens that you may want to refer to again.

The **Search** tab opens a search facility you can use, as shown below. In this example we typed 'saving pictures' in the **Type in the keyword to find** text field and clicked the **List Topics** button. Then, selecting one of the topics found and clicking **Display**, opened Help information on it.

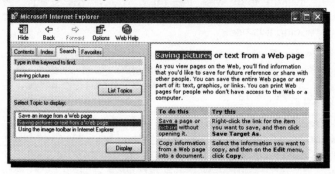

Fig. 3.19 Using the Help Search Facility

The Help provided by Microsoft with version 6 of the browser leaves much to be desired, but there is also more help available from their Web site, but you have to be prepared to struggle to find it.

Fig. 3.20 Microsoft's Product Support Web Site

To access product support from Microsoft as shown above you can use the **Help**, **Online Support** menu command and just follow the links. This, of course, will only work when you have your Internet connection open! Good luck.

4

More Skills and Features

As we saw in the last chapter, either Microsoft or your ISP will have provided a starting page for your Web browsing. These are, as you would expect, really professional pages with point and click links to other pages of interest. Some you can customise to show the type of information you are most interested in, and then make this your home page.

Fig. 4.1 A Typical Internet Service Provider's Home Page

You can also see in Fig. 4.1 above, an example of the advertising that is now a feature on many Web pages. The search engine pages are also weighed down with it. Generating advertising revenue certainly helps to pay for some of our 'free' Web facilities, but at the expense of speed. Every graphic has to be downloaded and takes valuable time.

A Useful Starting Site

When you get fed up with surfing between sites which offer all manner of visual and audio entertainment, you might like to visit one useful page we often revisit. Try entering the following address, which points to an American University site, so hopefully it will stay active. But don't forget things can change overnight on the Web.

www.ithaca.edu/Library/Training/useful.html

The header of this page is shown below. It is maintained by a librarian with a sense of humour and points to an interesting array of reference and other kinds of library oriented sites.

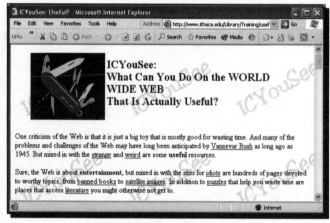

Fig. 4.2 A Useful Starting Site?

Using Web Information

Once you have found what you were looking for on the Web you can, with very little in the way of basic skills, save it to your own PC and use it for your own purposes. Most Web pages consist of code, text, graphic or video images, sound files, or links to files of some sort that have been used in the page construction. All of these can be saved for your own use, as we shall see (but don't forget copyrights).

The Mouse Pointer

In Windows, as with all other graphical based programs, using a mouse makes many operations both easier and more fun to carry out.

Explorer uses many different mouse pointers, with the most common illustrated below, which it uses for its various functions. When a program is initially started up probably the first you will see is the hourglass, which turns into an upward pointing hollow arrow. Some of the other shapes, as shown below, depend on the type of work you are doing at the time.

The hourglass which displays when you are waiting while performing a function.

The arrow which appears when the pointer is placed over menus, scrolling bars, and buttons.

The I-beam which appears in normal text areas of the screen.

The large 4-headed arrow which appears after choosing the **Control, Move/Size** command(s) for moving or sizing windows.

The double arrows which appear when over the border of a window, used to drag the side and alter the size of the window.

The Help hand which appears in the help windows, and is used to access 'hypertext' type links.

To see all the mouse pointers that are available to your system, click the Windows *start* button, open the Control Panel and double-click the **Mouse** entry to open the Mouse Properties dialogue box. If you then click the **Pointers** tab you will be able to scroll down the list of available pointers. If you find these too boring you could also look in the **Scheme** drop-down list and select from alternative pointer styles.

Copying Text

You can copy selected, or highlighted, text from an Explorer page to the Windows clipboard with the **Edit**, **Copy** menu command, the <Ctrl+C> shortcut, or the **Copy** Toolbar icon (if you have placed it on the Toolbar). If you want to copy all the text on a page, it is quicker to select it with the <Ctrl+A> keyboard shortcut, or the **Edit**, **Select All** command. The copied text will have any HTML tags stripped out, with the exception of any contained hyperlinks. These will still be active if the program you paste the text into supports them

Once the text you want is on the clipboard, you can **Paste** it, <Ctrl+V>, into whatever open Windows application program you want, and then save it. Notepad is useful for this, or WordPad for a lot of text. But remember, the text might look formatted in WordPad, but this is only done with imported space characters. In either case, you will almost certainly have to do some editing to remove lots of unwanted empty spaces.

Saving a Target Link

Explorer has a way of saving a Web file without you even having to open it. If you right-click your mouse pointer on a link in an open page, an object menu is opened, as we have seen before.

Selecting the **Save Target As** option from this menu, and completing the details of file name and destination folder in the **Save As** box, will start the download process. While this download is taking place a message window is opened with a progress bar that indicates how the process is proceeding, and shows an estimate of the remaining time that will be taken.

Viewing Source Code

If you want to see what the code for any page actually looks like, you can use the **View**, **Source** command. This opens

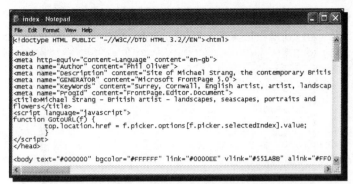

Fig. 4.3 Typical Source Code for Part of a Simple Web Page

the file in Notepad, so you can edit it as well and save it wherever you want, except back to its Web site, of course. Our example in Fig. 4.3 above shows some of the actual HTML source code for the Web page displayed on page 38.

Saving Whole Pages

There could be several reasons for wanting to save a whole Web page to your own disc drive:

- So that you can edit the source code to form the basis of a page of your own. Again don't forget copyrights.

- To create a hypertext 'reference book' of pages you have down-loaded. This would then work on any PC that had the files on it. Web based tutorials, maybe.

- To use embedded links in a file as instant Bookmarks.

Before version 5 of Explorer, you could not easily save whole Web pages, including their pictures, etc., to your hard disc. That has now changed, and you now have several options available from the Save Web Page box shown in Fig. 4.4, which is opened with the **File**, **Save As** menu command.

Fig. 4.4 Saving a Web Page to Disc

As shown there are four choices in the **Save as type** box, the first two allow you to save the whole Web pages.

Web Page, Complete (*.htm, *.html)

This is the most useful one which allows you to save the page to a folder on your hard drive. It will save the HTML page as one file, and all the graphics, audio and other contained files as other linked files on your disc. The links and references within the HTML page will be adjusted so as to refer to the new local locations of all the contained files saved on your hard drive.

You can then open the standard HTML file on your drive and the full page, with all graphics and extras will be loaded without requiring connection to the Internet.

Web Archive, Single File (*.mht)

This option is available if you have installed Outlook Express and lets you save an offline version of a Web page and all its contained graphics as a single archive '.mht' file. It seems that this file format is only used by Explorer 5 and Outlook Express 5 (and later), but it is useful if you want to send the page by e-mail.

Remember that the recipient must also be using the latest versions of Internet Explorer and Outlook Express. Unfortunately page backgrounds seem to get lost with this process.

Web Page, HTML Only (*.htm, *.html)

This option lets you save the current Explorer page with all the HTML codes still in place. A page saved in this way does not retain its graphics, only the text and codes. If you want to use the page again with your browser, but are not worried about the contained graphics, then save it this way.

Text File (*.txt)

This simply allows you to save the text from the page with all the HTML code stripped out. You might use this method to save the text of a whole Web page that you wanted to include in a word processor document.

Downloading a Program File

If you capture and work with graphics you may well need a program to quickly view and manipulate them. A good program we have come across to do this is Paint Shop Pro, and as an example we will step you through the process of downloading an evaluation copy of this from the Internet.

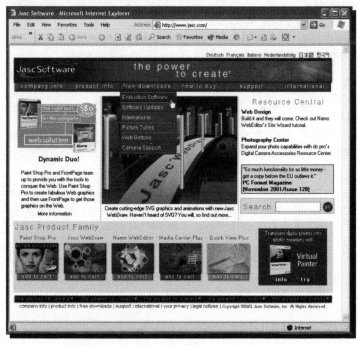

Fig. 4.5 Downloading an Evaluation Copy of Paint Shop Pro

To open the home page, shown above, type the following URL in the Address bar and press <Enter>:

www.jasc.com

Clicking **Evaluation Software** on the drop-down menu under **free downloads** opens a page for you to choose what software to download.

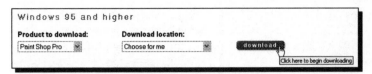

Fig. 4.6 Selecting what to Download

Choose Paint Shop Pro, or one of the others if you prefer, and click the **download** button shown in Fig. 4.6 above to

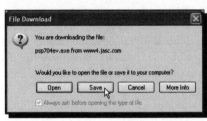

Fig. 4.7 The File Download Box

open the File Download box shown here in Fig. 4.7. Be aware that there is a danger of importing viruses if you download program files from an unknown source. The provider of this program should be a safe source, so click the **Save** button.

Complete the details in the **Save As** dialogue box, (we suggest you save it to a temporary folder called **Downloads**), and click **Save** to start the downloading process. This opens

Fig. 4.8 Monitoring the Process

the Saving box shown in Fig. 4.8, and as long as this box is open the downloading is still taking place. With a modem connection, this process took us well over an hour.

In our case above, a flurry of disc activity and the activation of the **Open** and **Open**
Folder buttons indicates the completion of the operation. We suggest you click the **Open Folder** button to check that the file has been received on your system.

Fig. 4.9 Checking the
Download

This should open the **Downloads** folder in a 'My Computer' window, and you should see the file **psp704ev** there as shown in our example on the left.

If you want to find out more about the file, you could right-click the mouse pointer on its icon and select the **Properties** option from the opened menu. This opens a tabbed dialogue box giving two pages of details about the file.

Once you have followed the online instructions and installed Paint Shop Pro you will have a very useful and powerful graphics and drawing program to evaluate. Of course, if you carry on using it you will have to pay a registration fee.

An Internet Software Source

A favourite site of ours for finding extra Internet and other software is run by the TUCOWS Network, and it is well worth

taking a look at one of their sites. If you are thinking of downloading anything from the Internet you should try and find the nearest site to you that you can so as to save on downloading time. Tucows (sorry about the name) have a mirror site at the following address in the UK:

www.mirror.ac.uk/sites/ftp.tucows.com/tucows

A few minutes looking around this site is well worth anybody's time. You can find some very powerful free and evaluation programs to download and try out.

Printing Web Pages

It was originally thought by some, that computers would lead to the paperless office. That has certainly not proved to be correct. It seems that however good our electronic communication media becomes most people want to see the results printed on paper. As far as books are concerned, long may that last!

Microsoft have built into Explorer 6 the ability to produce the best printed output of Web pages we have so far seen. There is a more powerful preview option, pages with frames are handled and you can also control the headers and footers that are printed. The screen layout of most Web pages with a text content depends on the size of the window you have open and the font size you are using. Try this out by viewing a text-based page full screen and then reducing it to a smaller window. Usually the page will be reformatted around any embedded graphics. The same thing happens when you print, except that the paper size, not the window, determines the eventual layout.

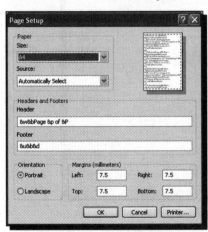

Fig. 4.10 The Page Setup Box

Before you print, you should check the page settings with the **File**, **Page Setup** menu command, which opens the dialogue box shown in Fig. 4.10. The usual options of paper **Size** and **Source**, **Margins** and **Orientation** are controlled here, as well as those of **Header** and **Footer**. The Help section, shown in Fig. 4.11 on the next page is perhaps the easiest way to come to terms with how to control the header and footer printing features.

In each **Headers** and **Footers** box, specify the information to be printed by using the following variables. Variables can be combined with text (for example, Page &p of &P).

To print this	Type this
Window title	&w
Page address (URL)	&u
Date in short format (as specified by Regional Settings in Control Panel)	&d
Date in long format (as specified by Regional Settings in Control Panel)	&D
Time in the format specified by Regional Settings in Control Panel	&t
Time in 24-hour format	&T
Current page number	&p
Total number of pages	&P
Centered text (following &b)	&b
Right-aligned text (following &b&b)	&b&b
A single ampersand (&)	&&

Fig. 4.11 How to Control Page Header and Footers

When you are ready to print, use the <Ctrl+P> key combination, or the **File**, **Print** menu command, to open the Print dialogue box shown in Fig. 4.12. If you use the **Print** Toolbar button the last Print settings will be used.

Fig. 4.12 The General Page of the Print Dialogue Box

Make sure the correct printer is selected, choose the pages to be printed, how many copies you want, how you want any page frames to print on the **Options** page (Fig. 4.13), and finally click **Print** to start the printing process. You should be impressed with the results, we certainly were.

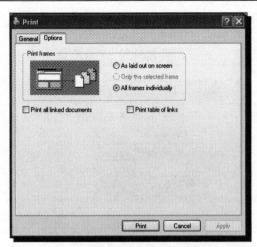

Fig. 4.13 The Options Page of the Print Dialogue Box

There are two very useful features in the **Options** page of the Print dialogue box, that we have not yet seen elsewhere:

*   The **Print table of links** option, which when checked, gives a hard copy listing of the URL addresses of all the links present in the printed Web page.

*   The **Print all linked documents** option, which not only prints the current Web page, but all those linked to it. This is a great way to print a whole Web site, as long as its links are not too deeply embedded.

Print Preview

A feature added to the previous version of Explorer allows you to preview your print output on screen. If you use this before printing you can get a good idea if it is worth attempting to print the page. As you may have found out, some Web pages just will not print properly. The results of using the **File**, **Print Preview** command with one of our Web pages are shown in Fig. 4.14 on the next page.

Fig. 4.14 A Print Preview of a Web Page

The toolbar lets you move between pages, zoom them in and out, open the Page Setup box and finally, when you are happy, lets you send the page to your printer.

The Media Bar

The new Media Bar enables you to play music, video, and mixed-media files from within the Explorer 6 browser. You can use it to listen to your favorite CD or radio station, or to go to **WindowsMedia.com** for more online media files.

To view the Media Bar simply click the **Media** button on the Toolbar. The Media Bar appears in the Explorer Bar pane. To resize an Explorer Bar pane within the browser window, move the pointer over the right edge of the pane until it changes to a double-headed arrow, and then drag the edge to the left to make the pane smaller, or to the right to make it larger.

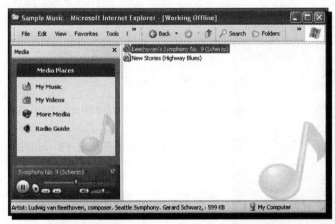

Fig. 4.15 Playing Sample Music on the Media Bar

As shown in Fig. 4.15 above, the Media Bar is divided into two sections. The top section provides links to any media files stored on your PC in the **My Music** or **My Video** folders. **More Media** and **Radio Guide** let you access the **WindowsMedia.com** Web site, where you can find and play online media files, such as music, radio stations, and movie and entertainment clips. The bottom section has the player controls which let you play, stop, adjust, and control the audio volume of media files, as shown in Fig. 4.16.

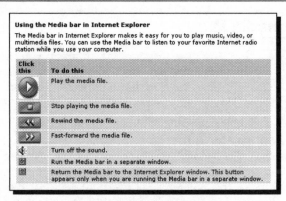

Using the Media bar in Internet Explorer

The Media bar in Internet Explorer makes it easy for you to play music, video, or multimedia files. You can use the Media bar to listen to your favorite Internet radio station while you use your computer.

Click this	To do this
▶	Play the media file.
◻	Stop playing the media file.
◀◀	Rewind the media file.
▶▶	Fast-forward the media file.
◀:	Turn off the sound.
▣	Run the Media bar in a separate window.
▣	Return the Media bar to the Internet Explorer window. This button appears only when you are running the Media bar in a separate window.

Fig. 4.16 The Media Bar Controls

The Media Bar includes a **Media Options** menu that enables you to quickly locate media files and set your Media Bar preferences. These can include, automatically playing media files in the Media Bar rather than another media player, or choosing a list of preferred types to play media. You also have the option to turn off the display of online media content in the Media Bar.

Fig. 4.17 Playing an Online Video

Our example in Fig. 4.17 shows the Media Bar online after the **More Media** button (see Fig. 4.15) was clicked. The top section of the bar shows the media options available at the time. We selected one of the **Video** links, and a poor quality advertising video about Las Vegas played jerkily in the section below.

For videos we don't think this feature is very useful, especially if you have to put up with a modem connection to the Internet. It is worth playing with the **Radio** section though.

History Files

Explorer stores all the Web pages and files you view on your hard disc, and places temporary pointers to them in a folder. In our case with Widows XP this was:

C:\Documents and Settings\Phil\Local Settings\History

You should not need to access this folder though, as to return to these in the future, first use the **File**, **Work Offline** command and then click the **History** icon on the Toolbar which opens the History Explorer bar, as shown below.

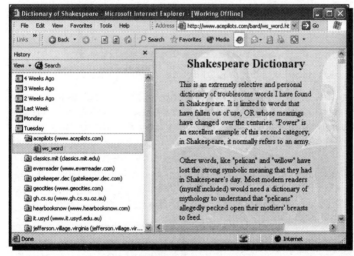

Fig. 4.18 Using the History Bar

In this vertical bar, you can scroll offline through the sites you have recently visited. Moving the pointer over the entries will open a banner giving details of the dates, or file locations involved. Clicking on a blue 'date' icon opens a list of the sites visited. Clicking on a site will open a list of the pages you accessed there, and selecting one of these will open it for you so that you can read it offline.

This is an excellent feature. If you pay for your Internet access by the minute, you needn't read Web pages when they are live, but just make sure they have completely downloaded, go offline and use the History Bar to work through them at your leisure.

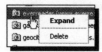

Right-clicking on any list item gives you the options to **Expand** or **Collapse** the list, or to **Delete** it, as shown here. This gives you the option of editing out any pages you don't want to keep in the list.

You can control the length of time that Explorer keeps this History information in the settings sheet that is opened with the **Tools**, **Internet Options**, command.

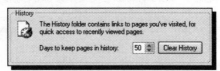

Fig. 4.19 Controlling the History Files

Ours was set for 50 days, as shown above, so all the saved History files expire 50 days after they were visited. This is obviously a personal setting and may depend on the size of

Fig. 4.20 Searching the History Bar

your hard disc. You can delete them all immediately by clicking the **Clear History** button, to release the hard disc space used.

You can now search through the files in your History list for a specific word or phrase, by clicking the **Search** button, typing the text wanted and finally clicking the **Search Now** button. An example of a single word search is shown Fig. 4.20. All the pages stored in the History that contain the text searched for are listed.

The **View** button, as shown here, gives you four ways of ranking the list in the History bar.

The Cache

You may have noticed that a Web page, especially one with lots of graphics, loads more quickly into Explorer if you have already recently viewed it. This is because all the pages and files you view are stored either in the History folder or in a cache folder on your hard disc, called 'Temporary Internet files'. The next time you access that page, depending on your settings, Explorer checks to see if the page has been updated before bringing it to the screen. If any change to the page has occurred, the new version is downloaded. If not, a cached copy is quickly retrieved. As with the History files, you control the cache, from the Options box which is opened with the **Tools**, **Internet Options** command.

Fig. 4.21 Controlling Temporary Cached Files

The Temporary Internet files section of the General settings tabbed sheet is shown in Fig. 4.21 above. Pressing the **Delete Files** button will clear the cache, which will very rapidly free up space on your hard disc. The **Settings** button will open the following control box.

Fig. 4.22 Controlling the Cache Settings

This shows the location of the Temporary Internet Files folder, and that Web sites by default are automatically checked for changes in every Explorer session. To guarantee that every day you visit a site you always view the most up to date version of Web pages this is a good setting.

 You can also press the **Refresh** button shown here, or the **F5** key to refresh the current page being viewed. If there is a newer version of the page on its server this will then be downloaded to your PC. This does not always work properly with 'framed' pages though.

If you are short of space on your hard disc, you can reduce the size of your cache by lowering the **Amount of disk space to use** slider. Again this will reduce the number of sites that can be cached, and may slow you down. If you have another hard disc you could also move the cache onto it by clicking the **Move Folder** button. The **View Files** and **View Objects** options lets you look in the cache.

Any operations you carry out on the files in your cache or History folders, such as moving or deleting them, may affect any settings you have activated in the **Favorites** sub-menu, as described in a later chapter.

Privacy and Cookies

Cookies sound like the sort of thing you could enjoy with a mug of coffee, but in our context they are small text files that some Web sites create when you visit them. They are placed on your computer and are used to store information which the Web site can use next time you visit it. Some people worry a lot about the privacy implications of this.

One important new feature of Internet Explorer 6 is how it handles 'cookie filtering'. It is now easier for you to see what Web sites are doing with cookies, to view their privacy statements, and to generally manage cookies.

By default, Explorer 6 will not allow the use of cookies from sites you do not navigate to, unless that site has pledged not to use cookies relating to your personal identifying data.

To quote from Microsoft's Web site:

"Explorer 6 uses P3P, the *Platform for Privacy Preferences Project*, an XML-based technology under development from the World Wide Web consortium. This standard enables Web sites to state their privacy practices in the P3P XML vocabulary. Then P3P-enabled software such as Explorer 6, can act upon those stated practices."

Explorer 6 uses the P3P encoded privacy statements to compare a site's practices to your user settings, and then decides whether to accept cookies from that site.

Six pre-configured cookie settings are available, which are easy to adjust. They are, Accept All Cookies, Low, Medium, Medium-High, High, and Block All Cookies. To do this, action the **Tools**, **Internet Options** command, click the **Privacy** tab and move the slider up for a higher level of privacy or down for a lower one. Fig. 4.23 below shows the **Medium** setting.

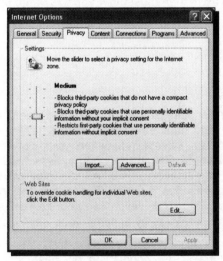

Fig. 4.23 Controlling your Privacy Settings

If you want to delete the cookies on your hard disc, go to the **General** tab of the above box and click the **Delete cookies** button, as shown in our Fig. 4.21.

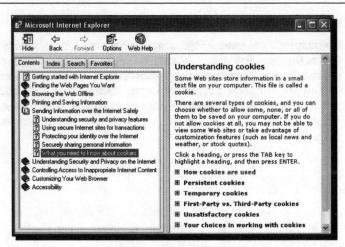

Fig. 4.24 Explorer Help on Cookies

To find out more about cookies we suggest you look in Explorer's Help files. There seems to be more information there about them than most other aspects of the software!

Security

Because of its design, the Internet itself does not provide security for any data transmitted across it. As we saw in Chapter 1, data travelling between your computer and a server somewhere else in the world passes through a large number of computer systems. An operator at any one of these computers has the potential to view, manipulate, or even corrupt, your data, which can thus be very susceptible to fraud or other misuse by unscrupulous individuals.

For most casual Web browsing this would not really matter, but if you are conducting business, doing Internet banking, or sending sensitive personal information, such as details of your credit card, you need security measures to make sure that your data is safe.

Explorer Security Measures

Netscape Communications originally developed a security technology called SSL, (short for Secure Sockets Layer protocol), which has become a standard since it was put into the public domain for the Internet community. This SSL protocol checks the identity of the server being accessed, carries out data encryption of any messages sent, and guarantees their general integrity. SSL is layered beneath the Internet application protocols (HTTP, Telnet, FTP, Gopher, etc.), but above the TCP/IP connection protocol. In this way it operates independently of the Internet protocols.

Microsoft Explorer supports SSL, as well as other security measures, which enable you to make secure credit-card purchases from a Web page. With these active on both your browser and the server you are transmitting to, your sensitive communications should be absolutely secure and unusable by third parties.

With Explorer you can tell whether a page or document comes from a secure server by looking at the status bar. If a padlock icon is placed there when the page is opened, the site is secure.

Security Zones

To help protect your computer from downloading or running possibly harmful files, Explorer 6 divides your browsing world into zones, and allows you to assign sites to a zone with a suitable security level. You can tell which zone a current Web page is in by looking at the right side of the status bar, as shown here. Whenever you attempt to open or download content from the Web, Explorer checks the security settings for that Web site's zone. There are four zones and by default, pages downloaded from a Web site are given the medium security settings associated with the **Internet zone**. Double-clicking on the Security rating on the status bar opens the box shown in Fig. 4.25 on the next page.

Fig. 4.25 Controlling Internet Security

This Security settings sheet is also opened with the **Tools**, **Internet Options** command. If you are worried about your system being 'contaminated' from a Web site, click the Restricted Sites button followed by the **Sites** button and give the problem site a **Restricted sites** rating.

A Secure Transaction

Internet banking has really caught on in the last year, and to encourage this trend most UK banks pay more interest on their Internet accounts. We have joined the rush and the next few screen examples were obtained while we were logging on to one of our online accounts.

Clicking a link to a secure site opens a Security Alert box, shown in Fig. 4.26, which warns you that you are about to enter a secure page. Perhaps 'warns' is the wrong word, as the message is more a reassurance than a warning.

Fig. 4.26 A Security Alert Message Box

You have the options to disable this warning for the future, as we have above, to get **More Info,** or to click **OK** to continue. .

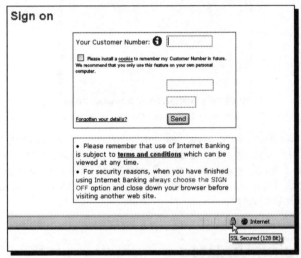

Fig. 4.27 Recognising a Secure Web Page

The above part page shows the padlock icon displayed in the status bar, indicating the Web page is secure. When you move the pointer over the padlock icon the level of site security is flagged as also shown above. By double-clicking the icon you can open a copy of the actual security certificate showing its properties.

You can also tell that the page is secure, by looking at the start of its URL in the Address bar; if it begins with 'https:' instead of 'http:', it is a secure page.

New Explorer Components

We saw in Chapter 2 that when Explorer 6 is installed on your PC a typical set of components is usually put there. These may work well for a long time, but eventually you will encounter a Web page that requires an Explorer component that you don't have. In fact with us the following box opened the first time we used the program.

Fig. 4.28 The Install On Demand Box

We needed the Java virtual machine component, but Explorer was offering to automatically download it for us. All we had to do was click the **Download** button, and a few minutes later all was well. This 'Install on Demand' feature really is excellent.

Keeping Updated

With more and more nasties like viruses coming along all the time, it is important that you keep Explorer, Outlook Express and Windows itself completely up to date. This way you can take advantage of the new protection and features that Microsoft are adding all the time. To do this, connect to the Internet, click the *start* button, followed by **Help and Support** and click the link **Keep your computer up to date with Windows Update**. Then just follow the online instructions. Some of the downloads may be quite large, so if possible do this early in the morning when the traffic across the Atlantic and in the US itself is a little quieter.

5

Where Shall We Go Today?

For anyone not involved with the Web, Microsoft's advertising catch phrase "Where do you want to go today?" was probably a bit confusing. For those that do a little surfing the confusion must be, how do we choose where to go?

You can literally spend hours following links from one place to another, and at the end of the day sometimes getting nowhere useful. Hence the term, surfing the Web! But if you want some specific information you will have to use one, or more, of the many search tools, or 'engines' that are available.

The Search Assistant

We introduced the **Search** button and bar earlier on page 19, when we did an initial search. What we used then was actually the Search Assistant, as shown here in Fig. 5.1.

When you open the Search bar, you have a selection of types of searches you can perform.

Find a <u>W</u>eb Page - Looks for specific web pages containing the searched-for information. Only two search engines were available to us when we last tried, UK Plus and MSN Web Search.

Fig. 5.1
The Search Bar

Previous searches - Locates information in the last ten searches you carried out. It displays the searches as a list of hyperlinks that you can follow to the returned search results.

Find a map - Searches for a place or address and tries to find a map for you. Only expedia.co.uk was available to us, which was not one of the better map sites for the UK!

At the bottom of the bar are three other items. **Files or Folders** and **Computers** open the Windows Search Companion in which you can search your own PC's hard discs, or if you are connected to one, your Intranet. The **People** option, as shown in Fig. 5.2, lets you search your own Address Book or some other online directory services.

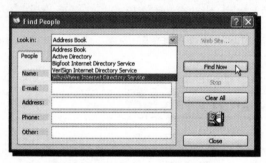

Fig. 5.2 Starting a Find People Search

To use any of these, you select it from the list and complete any 'question boxes' that are opened. The idea is very good, but the search tools offered in most of the options are very limited and in some cases not as good as those offered last year.

Customising the Assistant

If you click the **Customize** button on the Search bar a new window opens as shown in Fig. 5.3 on the next page in which you can, to some extent, control how the Assistant works.

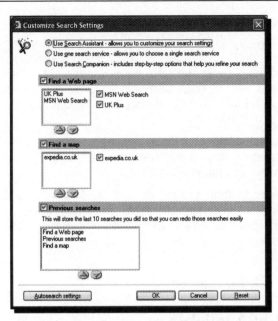

Fig. 5.3 Customising Your Search Bar Settings

You can only use the search engines that are available in the lists above. Hopefully they will be added to over time. The idea seems to be that you can select which engines are used for each type of search, and rank them as well. An excellent idea but not carried through to the end user. Perhaps we should say, "watch this space!" and also keep our fingers crossed. Mind you we have been doing that for over two years now!

Search Tools

There are a number of search tools, or engines, available to help you find what you want on the Web. Some search all the contents of documents, others only the file name. Most of them rank the search results in order depending on the number of times the searched-for words appear in a document, or on some other criteria.

Basically there are two types:

- Directories, like Yahoo, Open Directory and Lycos, depend on people to submit a short description to the directory with the URL for new sites, which are then reviewed. A search request to the directory then looks for matches only in the descriptions submitted.

- Search engines like Google, Alta Vista and Infoseek will find individual pages of a Web site that match your search, even if the site itself has nothing to do with what you are looking for.

Each search tool seems to use a different method of searching, so your search results may vary when you use different ones. Be patient as you may not always find what you're looking for very easily.

What is Available

In the next few pages we alphabetically list some of the main search tools that are available to you, with their URL addresses and a few comments on each. To access these you should type their URL into the Address bar and then click the **Go** button. You may find it useful to build up a list of search addresses as Favorites. The next chapter will show you how.

Be patient with the search tools, they are all different. With most you simply type in the text you want to search for, but they usually offer much more complicated searches as well. If you have problems, look for a Help link and spend a few minutes reading how best to use the site's facilities. Don't forget that these are changing all the time, and no Web listing can ever be fully current!

AltaVista

www.altavista.com

www.altavista.co.uk

One of the oldest search engines on the web, AltaVista opened in December 1995 and used to be one of our favourites. Seems to have lost its way of late, after several ownership changes.

AOL Search

search.aol.com

AOL Search (America On Line) allows its members to search across the web and in AOL's own portal content. Anyone can use the address listed above, but it does not list AOL content. Launched in October 1999.

Ask Jeeves

www.askjeeves.com

www.ask.co.uk

A human-powered search service that aims to direct you to the exact page that answers your question. If it fails to find a match within its own database, then it will provide matching web pages from various search engines. Opened fully on June 1, 1997.

FAST Search

www.alltheweb.com

Has one of the largest indexes on the Web, with well over 600 million pages. Fast's search results are provided to many other portal sites.

Google

www.google.com

Google is our favourite. At over 1.5 billion it offers the largest collection of web pages of any crawler-based search engine. It is very fast and makes heavy use of link analysis as a primary way to rank its result pages. In other words, the more people that link to a site, the higher will be its ranking. Google provides web page search results to a variety of partners, including Yahoo and Netscape Search. Google also provides the ability to search for images, through Usenet discussions and its own version of the Open Directory.

HotBot
www.hotbot.com
Another popular engine due to its large index of the Web. Owned by Lycos but run as a separate search service.

Inktomi
www.inktomi.com
The Inktomi index powers several other search services, such as HotBot. There is no way to query the Inktomi index directly.

LookSmart
www.looksmart.com
A human-compiled directory of web sites. As well as being a stand-alone service, LookSmart provides directory results to MSN Search and other partners. Inktomi provides it with search engine results when a search fails to find a match from among LookSmart's reviews.

Lycos
www.lycos.com
www.lycos.co.uk
In April 1999 Lycos changed to a directory model similar to Yahoo. Its main listings come from AllTheWeb.com and the Open Directory project.

MSN Search
http:// search.msn.com
Microsoft's MSN Search service is a LookSmart-powered directory of Web sites, with secondary results from Inktomi.

Netscape Search
http:// search.netscape.com
Netscape Search's results come primarily from the Open Directory and Netscape's own Smart Browsing database. Secondary results come from Google. At the Netscape Netcenter portal site, other search engines are also featured.

Open Directory
http://dmoz.org
The Open Directory uses volunteer editors to catalogue the Web. It was launched in June 1998 and then acquired by Netscape. AOL, Google and Lycos use Open Directory information.

SearchUK
www.searchuk.com
Automatically indexes UK related domains (.co.uk, etc.) and will include UK sites outside these domains (.com, etc.) as long as strong UK content is notified to them.

UK Plus
www.ukplus.co.uk
Features searchable reviews of UK sites, prepared by a team of journalists. Users can also perform a general search across the entire Web using Inktomi. UKPlus is owned by Associated Newspapers and launched in Jan 1997.

Yahoo
www.yahoo.com
Probably the most popular search service and is the largest human-compiled guide to the Web, employing about 150 editors. Yahoo has well over 1 million sites listed and supplements its directory results with those from Google.

Google.com - As an Example

We cannot include examples of all the search tools listed, but to give you an idea of their power we have dabbled with a Google 'Groups' search. For anyone starting to get to grips with the Usenet newsgroups this tool is essential. As we saw earlier, the address of the Google site is:

www.google.com

This opens the Google home page shown in Fig. 5.4 on the next page. This page sums up the whole site, it is simple and uncluttered, which leads to very rapid search results.

Under the site logo are four buttons, **Web**, **Images**, **Groups** and **Directory**, with the default set to **Web**. Typing a word or phrase into the text box below and pressing the **Google Search** button will search Google's index of the whole Web and present you with a list of what it considers to be the most suitable sites.

Fig. 5.4 The Google Search Engine Home Page

The **Images** button lets you search the Web for pictures. The **Groups** button opens the page shown below in Fig. 5.5 and gives you access to the last twenty years of Usenet group discussions.

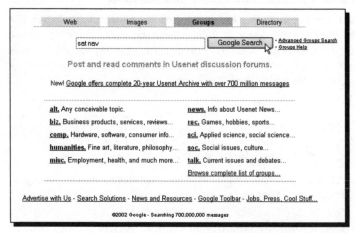

Fig. 5.5 Part of the Google Groups Starting Page

In case you were wondering, the **Directory** button gives you access to Google's version of the Open Directory (page 76).

You can browse the discussion (or Usenet) groups, or search them which is what we will do. We are interested in sailing and generally finding our way around the oceans, so we entered **sat nav** (satellite navigation) in the search box shown in Fig. 5.5 and then pressed the **Google Search** button. The first few of the 16,400 search results are shown in Fig. 5.6 below.

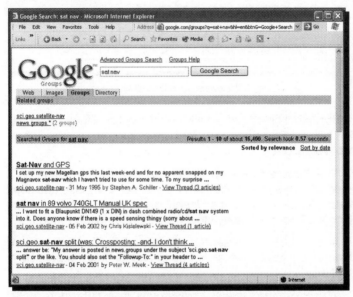

Fig. 5.6 An Initial Group Search Result

All of these entries are active links to news articles that have been posted in the last twenty years. We clicked the subject link for article 6 and read the posting (message), as shown in Fig. 5.7 on the next page.

Probably the content is not of much interest to many people in itself, but it's the principle we are trying to get over. You could work your way through the other messages in the retrieved listing, if you wanted, by clicking the **View:**

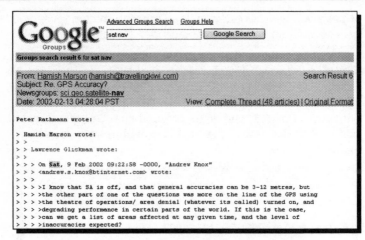

Fig. 5.7 Viewing an Individual Message

Complete Thread link which will locate any other messages in the same series, so that you can follow the whole 'conversation'.

The **Post a followup to this message** link below each message opens a window where you can compose and send your own message to the Usenet group, without even leaving Google. There is a fairly strict procedure to follow though.

In all, The Google search site is a very powerful and well thought out facility, which is free of charge. Let's hope it stays that way.

We cover the Usenet newsgroups in a little more detail when covering Outlook Express in a later chapter. You may find it useful to look at the introductory text there now, but exploring with Google Groups can be a very enjoyable and fast way of finding your way around Usenet.

6

Favorites and Working Offline

Using Favorites, which are Microsoft's version of Bookmarks (their spelling, not ours!) is an easy way to access the Web pages that you need to visit on a regular basis. It is much easier to select a page URL address from a sorted list, than to look it up and manually type it into the Address field.

Favorites

Fig. 6.1

With Internet Explorer, a Favorite is simply a Windows shortcut to a Web page.

When you first use Internet Explorer there may already be some Favorites available for you to use. Later, as your list of regular sites grows, your Favorites menu structure will grow too. In our example in Fig. 6.1, which was opened by clicking the **Favorites** option on the menu bar, we show how you can organise your lists of favourite bookmarks into a hierarchical list.

With Explorer 6 there are two ways of accessing your list of Favorites. From the menu bar, as shown above, and by clicking the **Favorites** Toolbar button. The latter method opens the Favorites list into an Explorer bar on the left of the Explorer window, as shown in Fig. 6.2 on the next page. This bar remains open until either the **Favorites** button or the X button on the top right of the Favorites bar are clicked.

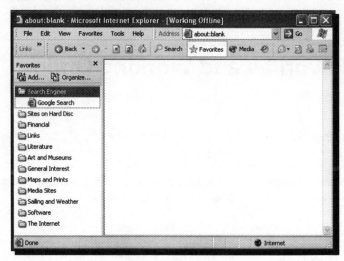

Fig. 6.2 The Favorites Bar Open

If you have a large enough monitor, or screen, you could easily work with this Favorites bar open all the time.

Adding a Favorite

There are several ways to add a Favorite to the menu. When you are viewing a Web page that you want to visit again, the

Fig. 6.3 Using the Object Menu

easiest method is to right-click on the page and select **Add to Favorites** from the object menu, as shown in Fig. 6.3. You can also use the **Favorites**, **Add to Favorites** menu command or, if the Favorites bar is open, click its **Add** button, as shown in Fig. 6.4. All these methods start the same procedure by opening the Add Favorite dialogue box also shown open in Fig. 6.4.

In the example we are adding a map page to our Favorite list. If your Add Favorite dialogue box does not show the list of folders, just click the **Create in** button which then opens the lower part of

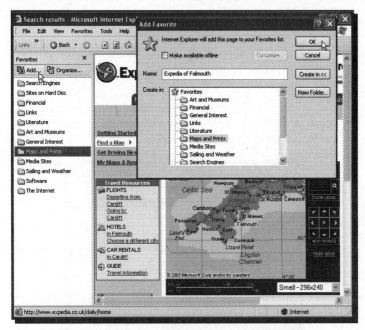

Fig. 6.4 A Composite Showing Ways to Add Favorites

the box, for you to select a folder to receive the new Favorite. Clicking the **OK** button then completes the process.

You could also simply click the **OK** button, without selecting a folder, to add the new Favorite to the bottom of the list. It would then appear at the bottom of your **Favorites** menu. The next time you open the **Favorites** menu that item should be there for you to use. Each time you add a Web page like this, the page's title is offered as the name of the Favorite, but it is easy to change this in the **Name** field of the Add Favorite box, or you can rename Favorites in the Organize Favorites window as described later.

Using Favorites

To open a Web page pointed to by a Favorite, you simply open the **Favorites** menu and click the item's name in the drop-down menu, or simply use the **Favorites** bar.

The Organize Favorites Window

You won't have to visit many pages before your **Favorites** menu will get very full and difficult to use. It is then time to tidy up a little.

You choose the **Favorites**, **Organize Favorites** command to open a box in which you can easily organise your Favorites, as shown below in Fig. 6.5.

Fig. 6.5 The Organize Favorites Box with a Folder Selected

This box has four buttons to **Rename**, **Delete** and **Move...** items or to **Create...** new folders, and has a very small navigation pane on the right.

When you click on a folder in the list, it opens to show the sub-folders and Favorites inside it, with a 'lined box' separating the selected links from the rest of the tree (it doesn't actually take you down a level); the Info pane on the left tells you where the folder is and when you last changed it.

When you click on a Favorite, the Info pane shows you its URL, when you last visited the page and how many times you have visited it. There is also a check box for making that page available offline. All these are shown in Fig. 6.6 on the next page for the new map Favorite we added earlier.

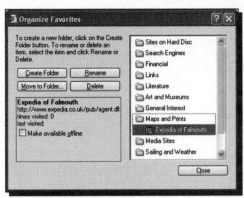

Fig. 6.6 The Organize Favorites Box with a Favorite Selected

You can select any item inside the 'lined box' and carry out any of the normal Windows editing functions from a right-click menu, but remember that actions carried out on a folder also affect the contents of that folder. If you delete a folder you will lose all its contents as well! There is a fail safe though, as deleted items are actually placed in the Windows Recycle Bin, as shown below.

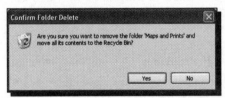

Fig. 6.7 The Warning Message Before you Delete a Favorite

Adding a New Folder

To add a new folder simply click the **Create Folder** button which places a new folder at the end of the current 'lined box' list, type the new folder name and press the <Enter> key. You can then drag any of your existing Favorites into this folder, or nest folders by simply dragging one into another. When you drag a Favorite or folder onto a folder in the list, it opens automatically in the navigation pane, to show you any sub-folders. As you drag, an insertion bar appears between items to show you where your dragged item will be placed.

Framed Pages as Favorites

Many Web pages these days are built using a framing technique, where one page may actually contain the content of several other pages set within 'frames'. This need not worry you too much, except that older versions of browsers could not properly save a framed page as a Favorite. Instead you were always given the front page of the site, rather than the particular page on the site you wanted.

With Explorer 6 this problem has mostly been solved. When you choose a framed page to save as a Favorite, as long as you don't use the right-click menu to create the Favorite, it will be saved in the correct position in its 'frameset', and the whole framed page will open correctly when you use the Favorite. If you use the right-click menu to make your Favorite, the page address saved is for the one that was present in the frame at that time.

The page titles do not process properly though, so you will need to change the titles of the Favorites as you save them to distinguish them from any others you save on the same site, or you will have several different Favorites all with the same name!

Links Bar Favorites

You have probably seen by now, that a Links folder is automatically placed in the Favorites list. The Favorites in this folder are the ones that show on the Links bar when it is

Fig. 6.8 The
Links Bar

opened. In Fig. 6.8 we show our default contents, but you can edit its contents the same as any other folder, which lets you put an easily accessible list of special Favorites in your control area. We have sometimes put links to some of our recently produced Web sites, so that we can quickly access them to review any changes.

Using Explorer Offline

Explorer 4 pioneered a way to help you keep up to date with your Web content. You could 'subscribe' to your favourite Web sites and have Explorer check them and automatically download new content to your hard disc, according to a schedule you specify. Explorer 6 calls this process working offline, as you can view these sites from your hard disc without being connected to the Internet.

If like us you access the Internet via a modem over a telephone line, you will probably want to save cost by being actualy online for as short a time as possible. With this scenario working offline has considerable advantage.

Viewing History Pages Offline

We saw on page 61 how you could use the History bar with the **File**, **Work Offline** command and view any pages still stored in your computer's caches. If you don't want to get more formal, and are prepared to keep your History files for long periods this may be the easiest method for you to work offline. There is a better method though, using Favorites.

Offline Favorites

Setting up an offline favorite to get Explorer to make a local copy of a site or page is very easy. You just go to the page

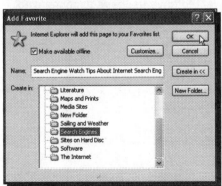

and choose **Add to Favorites** from the **Favorites** menu. Select the **Make available offline** option, as shown here in Fig. 6.9. Then click the **Customize** button to open the Offline Favorite Wizard shown next.

Fig. 6.9 Making a Favorite Offline

Fig. 6.10 The Offline Favorite Wizard's Second Box

This steps you through the procedure of choosing when to update the page and how much content to download.

After an introductory box, the one shown in Fig. 6.10 opens and gives you the options to just download the current page by selecting **No**, or to download the page and other pages linked to it. If you select **Yes** you can save whole Web sites to your hard disc. The number you select under **Download pages** controls the depth of links to download. Selecting '1' as above will download every page this Favorite is linked to. Selecting '2' will also download pages one level deeper. Be careful as you can easily fill your hard disc overnight!

The **Next** button opens the box shown in Fig. 6.11 in which you choose when you want to have the page 'synchronized'.

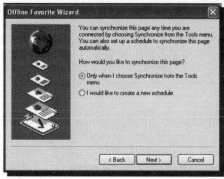

Fig. 6.11 Choosing Synchronisation Options

Synchronising is simply the process of checking that your saved page content is the same as that on the Web. If not, the new Web version is downloaded for you. If you select the option **I would like to create a new schedule** and then click **Next** the box in Fig. 6.12 below opens.

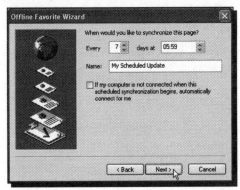

Fig. 6.12 Setting Synchronisation Times

Filling this box in is self explanatory, your choices determining when Explorer will automatically synchronise the page for you.

The last box in the Wizard (not shown) lets you give the password details for sites that may need them. When this is done clicking the **Finish** button will complete the wizard's operation and start the first synchronisation.

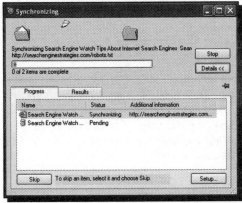

Fig. 6.13 Synchronising Our Favourite with its Web Content

In the future the Web page(s) on your hard disc will be updated automatically at the frequency you set, as long as your computer is actually switched on and connected at the time. If you use a modem connection, you may want to carry out this operation yourself with the **Tools**, **Synchronize** menu command, which opens the box shown below in Fig. 6.14. The choice is yours.

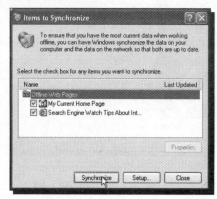

Fig. 6.14 Carrying Out a Manual Synchronisation

Working Offline

In the future, to view the saved pages without being connected to the Internet, use the **File**, **Work Offline** menu command, click the **Favorites** Toolbar button to open the Favorites bar and find the shortcut link in the list.

In this list any files available for offline viewing show in bold, whereas all the other links will be 'greyed out' as they are not available for offline viewing. Clicking the 'Search Engine Watch' link will open that page immediately. To open any of the other Favorites in the list you will have to connect to the Internet.

Favorite Properties

Every Favorite has a set of properties which you can edit quite easily from its Properties box, which is best opened for the first time from the Organize Favorites box.

Fig. 6.15 Opening the Properties Box

To do this, ensure the **Make available offline** option is selected, as shown above, and click the **Properties** button.

Fig. 6.16 An Offline Favorite's Property Box

As shown in Fig. 6.16, this set of Properties sheets gives you complete control of the Favorite and, as long as it has been selected for offline viewing, of its synchronisation schedule.

From the Schedule tabbed sheet you can choose for either manual or scheduled updates, and choose the update time and interval (1 to 99 days) and tell Explorer whether to dial up if you're not already connected to the Internet. Don't forget that your PC will still need to be switched on! From the Download tabbed sheet you can also choose how many levels of links to follow on the page, and whether to limit this to the same Web server or to set a size limit on the download.

The **Advanced** button lets you select any page elements you don't want to download, such as images, sound, video, ActiveX or Java components.

We will leave it to you to explore the further possibilities here. The big advantage of working offline is that once a page, or pages, have been downloaded and saved on your computer, you can view them all without even being connected to the Internet, by using the **File**, **Work Offline** command. This not only saves your phone bill if you use a modem, but also means the pages load up almost instantly.

Once a Favorite has been set up, the easiest way to control it is to right-click on it in the Favorite list, select **Properties** from the menu that is opened and make any changes you want in the Properties box that is opened.

7

E-mail with Outlook Express 6

Internet Explorer 6 comes with the very powerful mail and news facility, Outlook Express 6, built into it, which makes it very easy for you to send and receive e-mail messages. We are impressed with Outlook Express and use it for our e-mail correspondence.

What is E-mail

E-mail, or electronic mail, is cheaper, quicker, and usually much easier to prepare and send than Post Office mail. So what is an e-mail? It's simply an electronic message sent between computers which can include attachments like pictures, document files or Web pages. The message is passed from one computer to another as it travels through the Internet, with each computer reading its e-mail address and routeing it further until it reaches its destination, where it is stored in a 'mailbox'. This usually only takes a few minutes, and sometimes only seconds.

You can use e-mail for keeping in touch with friends and family and for professional reasons. You can send e-mail to most people, anywhere in the world, as long as they have their own e-mail address. These days all Internet service providers offer an e-mail address and mailbox facility to all their customers.

To retrieve your e-mail messages you have to contact your mailbox, download them to your PC, and then read and process them (just like any other mail). As we shall see, Outlook Express makes this whole procedure very easy and takes most of the mystery out of the whole e-mail process.

E-mail Addresses

An e-mail address usually has two main parts, which are separated with the '@' character, and usually contain at least one dot (the '.' character). The following is a typical, if short, example.

aperson@organisation.co.uk

The part before the @ is the user name which identifies him, or her, at the mailbox. This user name is usually made up from the name and initials of the user.

After the @ comes the domain name, which identifies the computer where the person has a mailbox and is usually the name of a company, a university, or other organisation. There is a central register of these domain names, as each must be unique. When you set up your account, you can sometimes get your service provider to customise a domain name for you, at a price, of course. Otherwise you will probably use the domain name of the service provider itself.

Next, there's a '.' or dot, followed by two, or three, letters that indicate the type of domain it is. In our example above this is **.co** which means the host is a business or commercial enterprise, located in the United Kingdom (**.uk**). In the USA, or anywhere else for that matter, this would be **.com** instead, but not followed by a country identifier.

A host name ending with **.edu** means the host is a US university or educational facility. A UK university would be **.ac.uk**. A **.org** indicates the host is a US non-commercial organisation.

Some of the more common extensions you might encounter are:

edu	Educational sites in the US
com	Commercial sites worldwide
gov	Government sites in the US
net	Network administrative organisations
mil	Military sites in the US

org	Organisations in the US that don't fit into other categories
fr	France
ca	Canada
uk	United Kingdom
**	Other county codes

Once you get used to these address parts, they begin to make more sense. For example, one of our e-mail addresses is

prmolive@csm.ex.ac.uk

This reads quite easily as:

PRM Oliver with connections to the Camborne School of Mines, part of the University of Exeter, which is an academic institution in the UK.

So if you know where somebody works you can even make an attempt to guess his, or her, e-mail address. A home address obtained through a commercial Internet provider would not be very easy though.

Two of our other e-mail addresses are

noel@kantaris.com
prmo@philoliver.com

Here we have established and registered our own domain names. They are both actually located on servers in the US. The Internet is International after all, but it still only takes seconds to download our mail.

Microsoft Outlook Express

Windows XP comes with the mail and news facility, Outlook Express 6, built into it, which makes it very easy for you to send and receive e-mail messages. The program should already have been added to your PC by **Setup** (an entry being placed on the **Start** menu left column). To start the program, left-click the menu option, shown here which displays the screen shown in Fig. 7.1 below.

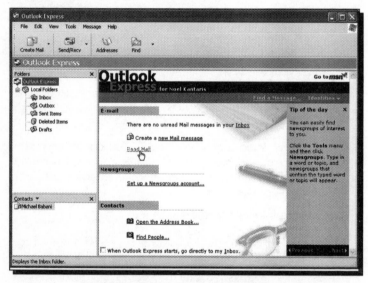

Fig. 7.1 The Outlook Express Opening Screen

Obviously, to send and receive electronic mail over a modem, you must make an arrangement with a commercial server. There are quite a few around now, and most have Internet options. Try and find one that is free or can provide you with a reduced rate for local telephone calls, to minimise your phone bills. Once you have registered with such a service, you will be provided with all the necessary information to enter in the Internet Connection Wizard, so that you can fully exploit all the available facilities.

Connecting to your Server

To tell Outlook Express how to connect to your server's facilities, you must complete your personal e-mail connection details in the Internet Connection Wizard shown in Fig. 7.2, which opens when you first attempt to use the Read Mail facility pointed to in Fig. 7.1.

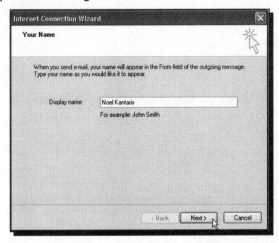

Fig. 7.2 The First Internet Connection Wizard Screen

If the Wizard does not open, or if you want to change your connection details, use the **Tools**, **Accounts** menu command, select the mail tab and click the **Add** button and select **Mail**.

In the first screen of the Wizard, type your name in the text box, shown above, and click the **Next** button to display the second screen, shown in Fig. 7.3 on the next page. Enter your e-mail address in the text box, if you have not organised one yet you could always sign up for free e-mail with Hotmail, the free browser-based e-mail service owned by Microsoft.

In the third Wizard screen enter your e-mail server details, as shown for us in Fig. 7.4. To complete some of the details here you may need to ask your Internet Service Provider (ISP), or system administrator, for help.

Fig. 7.3 The Second Internet Connection Wizard Screen

The details shown below will obviously only work for the specified person, so please don't try them!

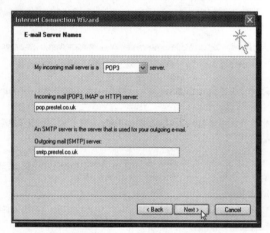

Fig. 7.4 The Third Internet Connection Wizard Screen

The next Wizard screen asks for your user name and password. Both these would have been given to you by your ISP. Type these in, as shown for us in Fig. 7.5, and click the **Next** button.

If you select the **Remember password** option in this box, you will not have to enter these details every time you log on. **BUT** it may not be wise to do this if your PC is in a busy office - for security reasons.

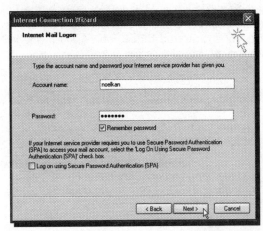

Fig. 7.5 The Fourth Internet Connection Wizard Screen

This leads to the final Wizard screen informing you of your success, which completes the procedure, so press **Finish** to return you to the Internet Accounts dialogue box, with your new account set up as shown below for us.

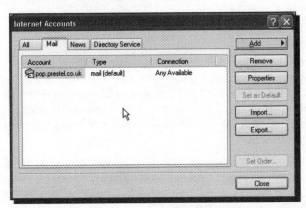

Fig. 7.6 The Internet Accounts Dialogue Box

In the future, selecting the account in this box and clicking the **Properties** button will give you access to the settings sheets (to check, or change, your details).

Once your connection is established, you can click the Read Mail coloured link, or the **Inbox** entry in the Folder List on the left side of the Outlook Express opening window. Both of these actions open the Inbox, which when opened for the first time, will probably contain a message from Microsoft, like that shown in Fig. 7.7 below.

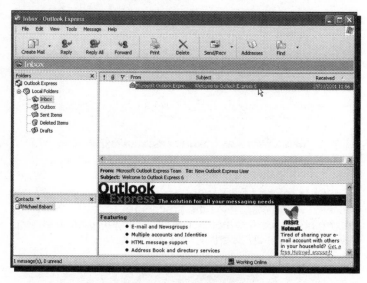

Fig. 7.7 The Inbox Outlook Express Screen

This shows the default Outlook Express Main window layout, which consists of a Folders List to the left with a Contacts list (from the Address Book) below it, a Message List to the right and a Preview Pane below that. The list under Folders contains all the active mail folders, news servers and newsgroups.

Clicking on one of these displays its contents in the Message List, and clicking on a message opens a Preview of it below for you to see. Double-clicking on a message opens the message in its own window.

A Trial Run

To check your mail, click the Send/Recv Toolbar icon which will connect you to the Internet and download any new messages from your mailbox. You can then read and process your mail at your leisure without necessarily still being connected to the Internet.

Before explaining in more detail the main features of Outlook Express we will step through the procedure of sending a very simple e-mail message. The best way to test out any unfamiliar e-mail features is to send a test message to your own e-mail address. This saves wasting somebody else's time, and the message can be very quickly checked to see the results. To start, click the Create Mail button to open the New Message window, shown in Fig. 7.8 below.

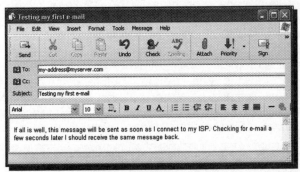

Fig. 7.8 Creating a New E-mail

Type your own e-mail address in the **To:** field, and a title for the message in the **Subject:** field. The text in this subject field will form a header for the message when it is received, so it helps to show in a few words what the message is about. Type your message and when you are happy with it, click the Send button.

By default, your message is stored in an Outbox folder, and pressing the Send/Recv button will connect to the Internet and then send it, hopefully straight into your mailbox. When Outlook Express next checks for mail, it will find the message and download it into the Inbox folder, for you to read.

The Main Outlook Express Window

After the initial opening window, Outlook Express uses three other main windows, which we will refer to as: the Main window which opens next; the Read Message window for reading your mail; and the New Message window, to compose your outgoing mail messages.

The Main window consists of a Toolbar, a menu, and five panes with the default display shown in our example in Fig. 7.7. You can choose different pane layouts, and customise the Toolbar, with the **View**, **Layout** menu command, but we will let you try these for yourself.

The Folders List

The folders pane contains a list of your mail folders, your news servers and any newsgroups you have subscribed to. There are always at least five mail folders, as shown in Fig. 7.9. You can add your own with the **File**, **Folder**, **New** menu command from the Main window. You can delete added folders with the **File**, **Folder**, **Delete** command. These operations can also be carried out after right-clicking a folder in the list. You can drag messages from the Message list and drop them into any of the folders, to 'store' them there.

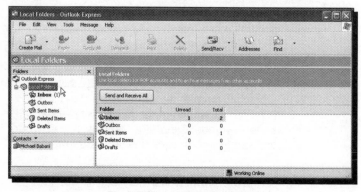

Fig. 7.9 The Local Folders Pane

Note the icons shown above; any new folders you add will have the same icon as that of the first added folder.

The Contacts Pane

This pane simply lists the contacts held in your Address Book. Double-clicking on an entry in this list opens a New Message window with the message already addressed.

The Message List

When you select a folder, by clicking it in the Folders list, the Message list shows the contents of that folder. Brief details of each message are displayed on one line, as shown in Fig. 7.10.

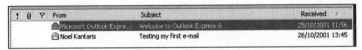

Fig. 7.10 Received Messages in Ascending Date Order

The first column shows the message priority, if any, the second shows whether the message has an attachment, and the third shows whether the message has been 'flagged'. All of these are indicated by icons on the message line. The 'From' column shows the message status icon (listed on the next page) and the name of the sender, 'Subject' shows the title of each mail message, and 'Received' shows the date it reached you. You can control what columns display in this pane with the **View**, **Columns** menu command.

To sort a list of messages, you can click the mouse pointer in the title of the column you want the list sorted on, clicking it again will sort it in reverse order. The sorted column is shown with a triangle mark, as shown in Fig. 7.11 below.

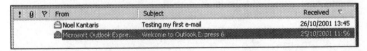

Fig. 7.11 Received Messages in Descending Date Order

As seen on the screen dump above, the received messages have been sorted by date, with the most recently received message appearing at the top. This is our preferred method of display.

Message Status Icons

This icon	Indicates this
0	The message has one or more files attached.
!	The message has been marked high priority by the sender.
↓	The message has been marked low priority by the sender.
☺	The message has been read. The message heading appears in light type.
✉	The message has not been read. The message heading appears in bold type.
✉	The message has been replied to.
✉	The message has been forwarded.
☐	The message is in progress in the Drafts folder.
✉	The message is digitally signed and unopened.
✉	The message is encrypted and unopened.
✉	The message is digitally signed, encrypted and unopened.
✉	The message is digitally signed and has been opened.
✉	The message is encrypted and has been opened.
✉	The message is digitally signed and encrypted, and has been opened.
⊞	The message has responses that are collapsed. Click the icon to show all the responses (expand the conversation).
⊟	The message and all of its responses are expanded. Click the icon to hide all the responses (collapse the conversation).
▽	The unread message header is on an IMAP server.
✉	The opened message is marked for deletion on an IMAP server.
▼	The message is flagged.
↓	The IMAP message is marked to be downloaded.
⊞↓	The IMAP message and all conversations are marked to be downloaded.
⊟↓	The individual IMAP message (without conversations) is marked to be downloaded.

Fig. 7.12 Table of Message Status Icons

The Preview Pane

When you select a message in the Message list, by clicking it once, it is displayed in the Preview pane, which takes up the rest of the window. This lets you read the first few lines to see if the message is worth bothering with. If so, double clicking the header, in the Message list, will open the message in the Read Message window, as shown later in the chapter.

You could use the Preview pane to read all your mail, especially if your messages are all on the short side, but it is easier to process them from the Read Message window.

The Main Window Toolbar

Selecting any one of the local folders displays the following buttons on Outlook's Toolbar.

Opens the New Message window for creating a new mail message, with the To: field blank.

Opens the New Message window for replying to the current mail message, with the To: field pre-addressed to the original sender. The original Subject field is prefixed with Re:.

Opens the New Message window for replying to the current mail message, with the To: field pre-addressed to all that received copies of the original message. The original Subject field is prefixed with Re:.

Opens the New Message window for forwarding the current mail message. The To: field is blank. The original Subject field is prefixed with Fw:.

Prints the selected message.

Deletes the currently selected message and places it in the Deleted Items folder.

Connects to the mailbox server and downloads waiting messages, which it places in the Inbox folder. Sends any messages waiting in the Outbox folder.

Opens the Address Book.

Finds a message or an e-mail address using Find People facilities of the Address Book.

The Read Message Window

If you double-click a message in the Message list of the Main window the Read Message window is opened, as shown below.

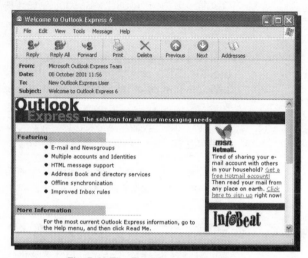

Fig. 7.13 The Read Message Window

This is the best window to read your mail in. It has its own menu system and Toolbar, which lets you rapidly process and move between the messages in a folder.

The Read Message Toolbar

This window has its own Toolbar, but only two icons are different from those in the Main window.

Previous - Displays the previous mail message in the Read Message window. The button appears depressed if there are no previous messages.

Next - Displays the next mail message in the Read Message window. The button appears depressed if there are no more messages.

Creating New Messages

We briefly looked into the creation of a new message and the New Message window earlier in the chapter (Fig. 7.8). However, before we activate this window again and discuss it in detail, let us first create a signature to be appended to all outgoing messages.

Your Own Signature

You create a signature from the Main window using the **Tools**, **Options** command which opens the Options dialogue box shown below when its Signature tab is selected and the **New** button is clicked.

Fig. 7.14 The Options Dialogue Box

You could also create a more fancy signature file in a text editor like Notepad, including the text and characters you want added to all your messages, and point to it in the **File** section of this box. You could choose to **Add signatures to all outgoing messages** which is preferable, or you could leave this option blank and use the **Insert**, **Signature** command from the New Message window menu system.

The New Message Window

This is the window, shown below, that you will use to create any messages you want to send electronically from Outlook Express. It is important to understand its features, so that you can get the most out of it.

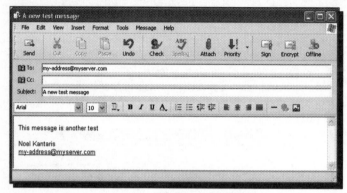

Fig. 7.15 The New Message Window

As we saw, this window can be opened by using the **Create Mail** Toolbar icon from the Main window, as well as the **Message**, **New Message** menu command. From other windows you can also use the **Message**, **New Message** command, or the <Ctrl+N> keyboard shortcut. The newly opened window has its own menu system and Toolbar, which let you rapidly prepare and send your new e-mail messages.

Message Stationery

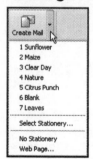

Fig. 7.16 Stationery

Another Outlook Express feature is that it lets you send your messages on pre-formatted stationery for added effect.

To access these, click the down arrow next to the **Create Mail** button in the Main window and either select from the **1** to **7** list, as shown here, or use the **Select Stationery** command to open a box with many more stationery types on offer.

The New Message Toolbar

The icons on the New Message Toolbar window have the following functions:

Send Message - Sends message, either to the recipient, or to the Outbox folder.

Cut - Cuts selected text to the Windows clipboard.

Copy - Copies selected text to the Windows clipboard.

Paste - Pastes the contents of the Windows clipboard into the current message.

Undo - Undoes the last editing action.

Check Names - Checks that names match your entries in the address book, or are in correct e-mail address format.

Spelling - Checks the spelling of the current message before it is sent, but is only available if you have Word, Excel, or PowerPoint.

Attach File - Opens the Insert Attachment window for you to select a file to be attached to the current message.

Set Priority - Sets the message priority as high or low, to indicate its importance.

Digitally sign message - Adds a digital signature to the message to confirm to the recipient that it is from you.

Encrypt message - Encodes the message so that only the recipient can read it.

Work Offline - Closes connection to the Internet so that you can process your mail offline. The button then changes to **Work Online.**

Message Formatting

Outlook Express provides quite sophisticated formatting

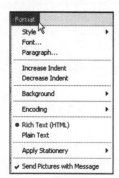

Fig. 7.17 The Format
Sub-menu

options for an e-mail editor from both the **Format** menu and Toolbar. These only work if you prepare the message in HTML format, as used in Web documents. You can set this to be your default mail sending format using the Send tab in the **Tools**, **Options** box.

To use the format for the current message only, select **Rich Text (HTML)** from the **Format** menu, as we have done here. If **Plain Text** is selected, the black dot will be placed against this option on the menu, and the formatting features will not then be available.

The Format Toolbar shown below is added to the New Message window when you are in HTML mode and all the **Format** menu options are then made active.

Fig. 7.18 The Format Toolbar

You should be able to prepare some very easily readable e-mail messages with these features, but remember that not everyone will be able to read the work in the way that you spent hours creating. Only e-mail programs that support MIME (Multi-purpose Internet Mail Extensions) can read HTML formatting. When your recipient's e-mail program does not read HTML, and many people choose not to, the message appears as plain text with an HTML file attached.

Note: At the risk of being called boring we think it is usually better to stick to plain text without the selection of any message stationery; not only can everyone read it, but it is much quicker to transmit and deal with.

Using E-mail Attachments

If you want to include an attachment to your main e-mail message, you simply click the **Attach** Toolbar button in the New Message window, as shown in Fig. 7.19 below.

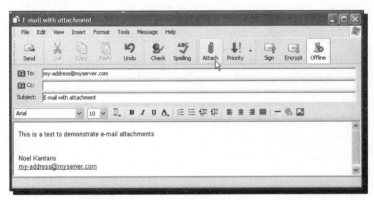

Fig. 7.19 Adding an Attachment to an E-mail

This opens the Insert Attachment dialogue box (Fig. 7.20), for you to select the file, or files, you want to go with your message.

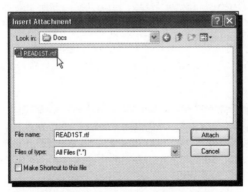

Fig. 7.20 The Insert Attachment Dialogue Box

In Outlook Express the attached files are placed below the **Subject** text box. In Fig. 7.21 we show two attachments, each with a distinctive icon that tells the recipient what each file is; the first a graphics .jpg file, the second a text .rtf document. It is only polite to include in your e-mail a short description of what the attachments are, and which applications were used to create them.

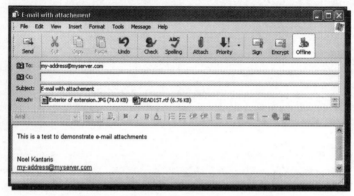

Fig. 7.21 Adding an Attachment to an E-mail

Clicking the **Send** icon on the Toolbar, puts each e-mail (with its attachments, if any) in Outlook's **Outbox** folder. Next time you click the **Send/Recv** Toolbar icon, Outlook Express connects to your ISP and sends all the e-mails stored in it.

Receiving Attachments with an E-mail

To demonstrate what happens when you receive an e-mail with attachments, we sent the above e-mail to our ISP, then a minute or so later we received it back, as shown in Fig. 7.22 on the next page.

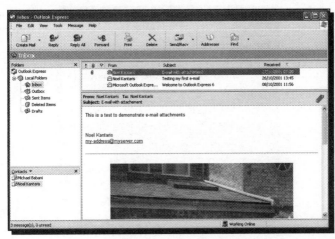

Fig. 7.22 A Received E-mail with Attachments

Note that the received e-mail shows the graphics (.jpg) file open at the bottom of the Preview pane, but there is no indication of any other attachments. To find out how many attachments were included with the received e-mail, double-click the e-mail to open it in its own window and reveal all of them in the **Attach** box shown in Fig. 7.23 below.

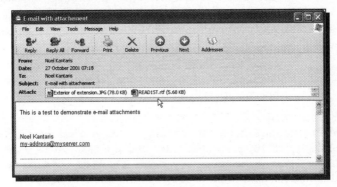

Fig. 7.23 An E-mail Opened in its Own Window

To view or save an attachment file, left-click its entry on the list. This opens the virus Warning box shown in Fig. 7.24.

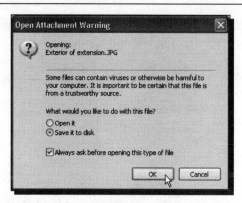

Fig. 7.24 The Open Attachment Warning Window

Each attached file can be saved, opened in situ, or saved to disc by selecting **Open it** or **Save it to disk** from this box.

Replying to a Message

When you receive an e-mail message that you want to reply to, Outlook Express makes it very easy to do. The reply address and the new message subject fields are both added automatically for you. Also, by default, the original message is quoted in the reply window for you to edit as required.

With the message you want to reply to still open, click the Reply to Sender Toolbar icon to open the New Message window and the message you are replying to will, by default, be placed under the insertion point.

With long messages, you should not leave all of the original text in your reply. This can be bad practice, which rapidly makes new messages very large and time consuming to download. You should usually edit the quoted text, so that it is obvious what you are referring to. A few lines may be enough.

Removing Deleted Messages

Whenever you delete a message it is actually moved to the Deleted Items folder. If ignored, this folder gets bigger and bigger over time, so you need to check it frequently and

manually re-delete messages you are sure you will not need again.

If you are confident that you will not need this safety net, you can opt to **Empty messages from the 'Deleted Items' folder on exit** in Maintenance tab settings of the **Tools**, **Options** box, opened from the Main window, as shown in Fig. 7.25.

Fig. 7.25 Cleaning up Messages

Organising your Messages

Perhaps most of the e-mail messages you get will have no 'long term' value and will be simply deleted once you have dealt with them. Some however you may well need to keep for future reference. After a few weeks it can be surprising how many of these messages can accumulate. If you don't do something with them they seem to take over and slow the whole process down. That is the reason for the Folders List.

As we saw earlier you can open and close new folders in this area, and can move and copy messages from one folder into another.

Fig. 7.26 Moving a
Message

To move a message, you just select its header line in the Message List and with the left mouse button depressed 'drag' it to the folder in the Folders List, as shown in Fig. 7.26. When you release the mouse button, the message will be moved to that folder.

The copy procedure is very much the same, except you must also have the <Ctrl> key depressed when you release the mouse button. You can tell which operation is taking place by looking at the mouse pointer. It will show a '+' when copying, as on the right.

The System Folders

Outlook Express has five folders which it always keeps intact and will not let you delete. Some of these we have met already.

The *Inbox* holds all incoming messages; you should delete or move them from this folder as soon as you have read them.

The *Outbox* holds messages that have been prepared but not yet transmitted. As soon as the messages are sent they are automatically removed to the *Sent Items* folder. You can then decide whether to 'file' your copies of these messages, or whether to delete them. As we saw earlier, deleted messages are placed in the *Deleted Items* folder as a safety feature.

The *Drafts* folder is used to hold a message you closed down without sending it - the program will ask you whether to save such a message in this folder. We also use the Drafts folder to store our message pro-formas and unfinished messages that will need more work before they can be sent.

8

Some Other E-mail Features

Spell Checking

Many of the e-mail messages we receive seem to be full of errors and spelling mistakes. Some people do not seem to read their work before clicking the 'Send' button. With Outlook Express this should be a thing of the past, as the program is linked to the spell checker that comes with other Microsoft programs. If you do not have any of these, the option will be greyed out, meaning that it is not available.

To try it out, prepare a message in the New Message window, but make an obvious spelling mistake, maybe like ours below. Pressing the Spelling Toolbar button, the **F7** function key, or using the **Tools, Spelling** menu command, reveals the drop-down sub-menu shown below in Fig. 8.1.

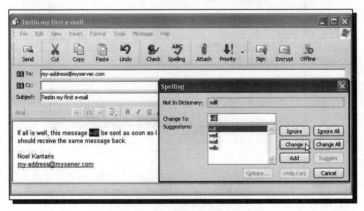

Fig. 8.1 Using the Spell Checker

Any words not recognised by the checker will be flagged up as shown. If you are happy with the word just click one of the **Ignore** buttons, if not, you can type a correction in the **Change To:** field, or accept one of the **Suggestions:**, and then click the **Change** button. With us the **Options** button always seemed 'greyed out', but you can get some control over the spell checker on the settings sheet opened from the main Outlook Express menu with the **Tools**, **Options** command, and then clicking the Spelling tab.

The available options, as shown in Fig. 8.2, are self-explanatory so we will not dwell on them. If you want every message to be checked before it is sent, make sure you select the **Always check spelling before sending** option.

Fig. 8.2 The Options Spelling Dialogue Box

In the above dialogue box, you could also choose to have the Spell Checker ignore **Words with numbers**, if you so wish, before clicking the **Apply** button.

Connection at Start-up

While you are looking at the program settings, open the
Connection tabbed sheet, shown in Fig. 8.3.

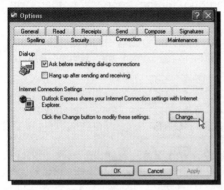

Fig. 8.3 The Options Connection
Dialogue Box

This gives you some
control of what
happens when you
open Outlook
Express, depending
on your connection
settings for Internet
Explorer. If you have
a modem
connection to the
Internet, it can be
annoying when a
program goes into
dial-up mode un-
expectedly. To look
at these settings, click the **Change** button which displays the
dialogue box in Fig. 8.4 below.

Fig. 8.4 The Internet Properties Dialogue Box

Next, select the **Never dial a connection** option so that you only 'go on line' (as long as you have not chosen to **Work Offline** from the **File** menu option), when you click  the Send/Recv toolbar icon shown here. If you have more than one Internet connection, the down arrow to the right of the icon lets you select which one to use.

If, on the other hand, you have a permanent Internet connection, you might like to deselect the **Never dial a connection** option.

Printing your Messages

It was originally thought by some, that computers would lead to the paperless office. That has certainly not proved to be correct. It seems that however good our electronic communication media becomes most people want to see the results printed on paper. As far as books are concerned, long may that last!

Outlook Express 6 lets you print e-mail messages to paper, but it does not give you any control over the page settings it uses. You can, however, alter the font size of your printed output as it depends on the font size you set for viewing your messages. As shown here in Fig. 8.5, you have five 'relative' size options available from the **View**, **Text Size** menu command.

When you are ready to print a message in the Read Message window, use the

Fig. 8.5 The View Menu.

<Ctrl+P> key combination, or the **File**, **Print** menu command, to open the Print dialogue box shown in Fig. 8.6 on the next page with its General tab selected.

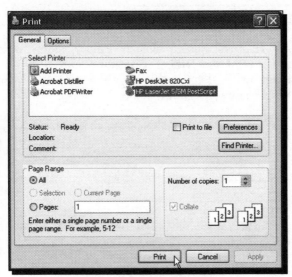

Fig. 8.6 The Print Dialogue Box

Make sure the correct printer, **Page Range**, and **Number of copies** you want are selected, then click **Print**. You can also start the printing procedure by clicking the Print Toolbar icon shown here.

If the message has Web page links on it, there are two useful features in the Options tab of the Print dialogue box shown above. These are:

- The **Print all linked documents** option, which when checked not only prints the message, but also all the Web pages linked to it.

- The **Print table of links** option, which when checked, gives a hard copy listing of the URL addresses of all the links present in the page.

Outlook Express Help

Outlook Express has a built-in Help system, which is accessed with the **Help**, **Contents and Index** menu command, or the **F1** function key. These open a Windows type Help window, as shown in Fig. 8.7 below.

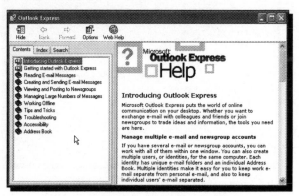

Fig. 8.7 The Outlook Express Help System.

We strongly recommend that you work your way through all the items listed in the **Contents** tabbed section. Clicking on a closed book icon will open it and display a listing of its contents. Double-clicking on a list item will then open a window with a few lines of Help information.

Another way of browsing the Help system is to click the **Index** tab and work your way through the alphabetic listing. The **Search** tab, on the other hand, opens a search facility you can use by typing your query in the **Type in the keyword to find** text field and clicking the **List Topics** button, then selecting one of the topics found and clicking **Display** to open Help information on it.

The Help provided by Microsoft with Outlook Express, is an improvement over some earlier versions of the program, and it is well worth spending some time getting to grips with it. If you are connected to the Internet, the Web Help icon accesses the Support Online from Microsoft Technical Support, which can give more specific help with the program.

The Address Book

E-mail addresses are often quite complicated and not at all easy to remember. With Outlook Express there is a very useful Address Book built in and accessed by clicking the menu icon with the same name. Below in Fig. 8.8, we show part of an example.

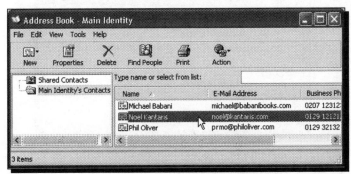

Fig. 8.8 The Address Book Screen

Once in the Address Book, you can manually add a person's full details and e-mail address, in the Properties box that opens when you click the New Toolbar icon and select **New Contact**, as shown here. Selecting **New Group** from this drop-down menu lets you create a grouping of e-mail addresses, you can then send mail to everyone in the group with one operation.

To send a new message to anyone listed in your Address Book, open a New Message window and use the **Tools**, **Select Recipients** command, or click on any of the **To:** or **Cc:** icons shown here on the left.

In the Select Recipients box which is opened (Fig. 8.9), you can select a person's name and click either the **To:->** button to place it in the **To:** field of your message, the **Cc:->** button to place it in the **Cc:** field, or the **Bcc:->**button to place it in the **Bcc:** field.

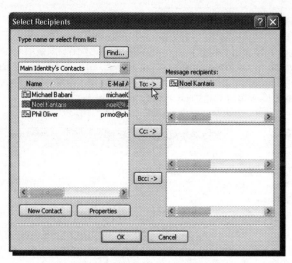

Fig. 8.9 The Select Recipients Screen.

The **New Contact** button lets you add details for a new person to the Address Book, and the **Properties** button lets you edit an existing entry, as shown in Fig. 8.10 below.

Fig. 8.10 A Recipient's Properties Screen

Exporting and Importing an Address Book

Amongst the most valuable assets you might have on your old computer is your Address Book. After all, you have spent endless hours (over a period of time) compiling it and the last thing you want is to lose it, either because you are changing computer or because of some mishap.

Outlook Express has the facility to export your Address Book from your old computer, then import it into your new one. The same method can also be used to make a backup of your Address Book.

In your old computer, start Outlook Express, then in the Address Book:

- Use the **File**, **Export** command and click the **Address Book (WAB)** option.

- In the displayed Select Address Book File to Export to dialogue box, type a suitable name in the **File name** box and click the **Save** button.

In your new computer, start Outlook Express, then in the Address book:

- Use the **File**, **Import** command and click the **Address Book (WAB)** option.

- In the displayed Select Address Book File to Import from dialogue box, locate the drive and file holding your Address Book information and click the **Open** button.

A few seconds later, Outlook express displays the very welcome message shown in Fig. 8.11:

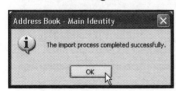

Fig. 8.11 A Welcome Message

It takes less time to do than to read how to do it, and you can save yourself hours of work and frustration! Go on, do it.

Address Book Help

We will leave it to you to find your way round this very comprehensive facility. Don't forget that it has its own Help system that you can use with the **Help**, **Contents and Index** menu command. An example section is shown open here in Fig. 8.12.

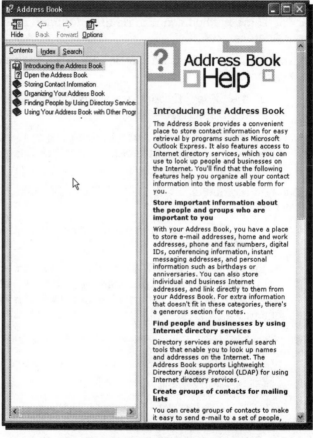

Fig. 8.12 The Address Book Help System

Using Message Rules

If you are ever in the situation of receiving e-mail messages from a source you do not want to hear from, you can use Message Rules to filter your incoming messages. Unwanted ones can be placed in your Deleted Items folder straight away. It can also be useful for sorting incoming messages and automatically routing them to their correct folders.

To open this feature, which is shown below, use the **Tools**, **Message Rules**, **Mail** menu command and select the criteria you want your incoming messages to be processed by.

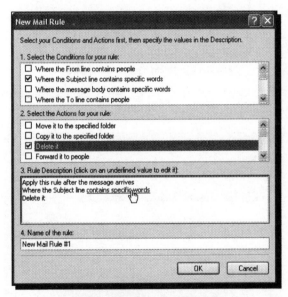

Fig. 8.13 Creating Message Rules, Box 1

In the first box, shown in Fig. 8.13 above, you select the conditions for the new rule. In box 2 you control what actions are taken, and the new rule itself is automatically 'built' for you in box 3. If you use this feature much you will probably want to name each of your rules in box 4.

In Fig. 8.13 on the previous page, we have set to intercept and delete messages which contain certain words in their Subject Lines. To complete the rule we clicked on the 'contains specific words' link and filled in the following dialogue box, clicking the **Add** button after each phrase.

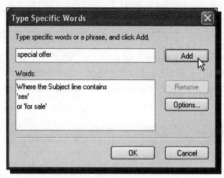

Fig. 8.14 Entering Words to Act Upon

When finished clicking on **OK** twice opens the Message Rules box shown in Fig. 8.15 below.

Fig. 8.15 The Message Rules Box

In this box you can control your rules. You can set multiple rules for incoming messages and control the priority that messages are sorted in the list. The higher up a multiple list a condition is the higher will be its priority.

If an incoming message matches more than one rule, then it is sorted according to the first rule it matches in your list.

Blocked Senders List

With Outlook Express 6 there is a very easy way to prevent messages from a problem source ever disturbing your peace again. When you first receive such a message, select it in the Messages List and action the **Message**, **Block Sender** menu command, as we did in the example below.

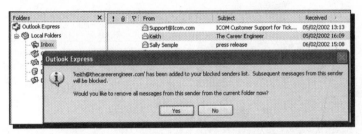

Fig. 8.16 Blocking Messages from a Single Source

This can be a very powerful tool, but be careful how you use it. If you are not, you may block messages that you really would rather have received!

The **Message**, **Create Rule from Message** menu command is a quick way to start the New Rule process, as the details of the currently selected message are automatically placed in the New Mail Rule box for you.

People that send mass junk mailings often buy lists of e-mail addresses and once you are on a list you can be sure that your mailbox will never be empty again! With these tools at your disposal you should only ever receive 'junk mail' once from any particular source.

msn Hotmail

If you don't have a mail account with an Internet Service Provider you can always use one of the free HTTP (Hypertext Transfer Protocol) services like Hotmail (now owned by Microsoft), where your messages are stored on a server as Web pages. Using it you can access your e-mail from any computer with an Internet connection, anywhere in the world.

You have to be live to sign up with Hotmail, so you may have to do it from work, or a friend's PC, or a Cyber Cafe. You can't do this any more from Outlook Express itself, so open Internet Explorer and enter the following URL into the Address box:

   www.hotmail.com

This opens the Hotmail home page shown in Fig. 8.17 below.

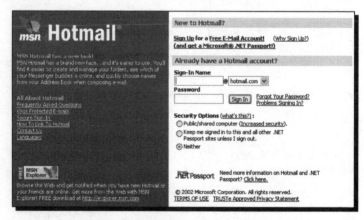

Fig. 8.17 The msn Hotmail Opening Web Page

For a full description of Hotmail's facilities you can use the **All about Hotmail** links on the left. To open a new and free e-mail account click the **Sign up** link under the **New to Hotmail?** heading and fill in the details requested. In our case and after about only five minutes we were registered, as shown in Fig. 8.18.

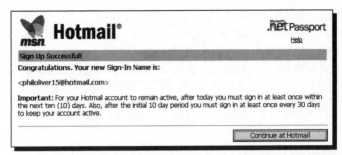

Fig. 8.18 Our Sign Up Successful Screen

As can be seen above, with Hotmail you have to use it, or you will lose it! The **Continue at Hotmail** button passes you through some unwelcome advertising screens and finally to the e-mail site shown in Fig. 8.19.

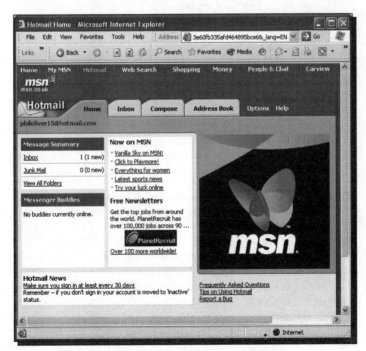

Fig. 8.19 Our Individual Hotmail Home Page

That's as far as we will go with Hotmail. If you are interested, you can explore and learn more by using the e-mail features.

We suggest you set your Hotmail home page as one of your Favorites. That way it is very easy to access it in the future. You could also use it to carry on ❤ Hotmail Home   with your Web surfing when you have checked your messages. Good luck.

Mailing Lists

When you start using e-mail you will probably want to receive lots of messages, but until your friends get active there is often a lull. This may be the time to join a mailing list.

Mailing lists are automatic mailing systems where a message sent to a list address is automatically sent on to all the other members of the list. The programs that manage this automatic mailing have names like Listserv, or Majordomo, which usually form part of the List address. Some of these lists are moderated and work much like journals, where submissions are accepted, sometimes edited, and then forwarded to subscribers. Others, however, have no constraints put on their contents! Although the quality and quantity vary from list to list, you can often find a wealth of free information in them.

To subscribe to a list, you need to know the name of the list and its address. Commands can vary between different lists, but they often follow the format given below. Note that there is a difference between the address to which you send postings, or messages, for the list, and the address you use for subscribing to it. Be sure to distinguish between these two addresses. One of the most common mistakes made by new Internet users is to send subscription requests to list addresses, which are then forwarded to all the members on the list. Please don't make this mistake, it can be annoying and time consuming for other list readers.

Finding a Suitable List

There are literally thousands of Mailing lists which you can join, covering almost every subject imaginable, from science, to art, to hobbies, and of course to any type of kinky sex. One of the biggest problems is finding the ones for you. Fortunately, there are several Web sites which give details of Mailing lists. A good one we have used, with lists grouped by topic, should be found at:

http://paml.net/indexes.html

This will put you in direct contact with your selected lists, where you will get instructions on how to subscribe and proceed. Make sure you keep a copy of any instructions, you will need them in the future, if you want to unsubscribe, or change your subscription details.

Typical Subscription Commands

All of these commands go to the subscription address:

sub *listname First Last*	To subscribe to *listname*, with your *First* and *Last* names given.
signoff *listname*	To unsubscribe from a list.
set *listname* **nomail**	To turn off mail from a list if you are going away.
set *listname* **mail**	To turn the mail back on when you return.

Once you have mastered Mailing lists you need never have an empty mailbox again. In fact you may find them to be a little overpowering, but lists can be a great source of up-to-date information.

Often Used E-mail Symbols

Once you start receiving messages from lists and other places around the globe, you may encounter some of the following acronyms, and symbols, which people often use to relieve the general boredom of life.

Acronyms

Btw	By the way
cu	See you (bye)
Faq	Frequently asked question
fyi	For your information
imho	In my humble opinion
imo	In my opinion
Rotfl	Rolling on the floor laughing
rtfm	Read the manual!
Ttyl	Talk to you later

Smileys

You tilt your head sideways to see them:

:-)	Smiling
:-D	Laughing
;-)	Winking
:-O	Surprise
:-(	Frowning, Sad
:-I	Indifferent
:-/	Perplexed
:-{)	Smiley with a moustache
8-)	Smiley with glasses
<:-|	Dunce
:-X	My lips are sealed
:->	Sarcastic

If these appeal to you try the *Unofficial Smiley Dictionary at:*

www.cosy.sbg.ac.at/doc/eegtti/eeg_286.html

9

News with Outlook Express 6

Discussion groups, or 'newsgroups', are a main feature of the Internet and are easily accessed with Outlook Express. They are often known as Usenet groups and consist of many thousands of separate news groups which let you actively take part in discussion on a vast number of topics. In fact almost any subject you could think of is covered, and the number of groups is growing larger all the time.

Outlook Express is a program you can use for viewing, and posting (or mailing), messages to these Usenet groups. Unlike e-mail, which is usually 'one-to-one', newsgroups could be said to be 'one-to-many'.

How Usenet Works

Usenet messages are shipped around the world, from host system to host system, using one of several available protocols, that you don't need to bother too much about. Your host server stores all of its Usenet messages in one place, which everybody with an account on the system can access, if they want. That way, no matter how many people actually read a given message, each host has to store only one copy of it. The host systems contact each other regularly and bring themselves up to date with the latest Usenet messages, sometimes this happens thousands of times a day.

Usenet is huge. We once saw it quoted that every day Usenet users transmit over 60 million characters into the system. Some of this information has to be of use! In fact there are so many active groups now, it is unlikely that your server will handle more than a fraction of them. This can be frustrating, if you keep seeing references to a group that you cannot access through your server.

Usenet Newsgroups

The basic building block of Usenet as we have seen is the newsgroup, which is a collection of messages with a related theme. These are arranged in a particular hierarchy that originated in the early 80s. Newsgroup names start with one of a series of broad topic names. For example, newsgroups beginning with '**sci**' should have scientific and engineering content. These broad topics are followed by a series of more specific topic names. '**sci.engr**' groups, for example, are limited to discussion about engineering subjects, and '**sci.engr.mining**' would be a group dedicated to very specific discussion on mining engineering topics.

There are many national and regional groups, including **uk**, but some of the main topic headers are:

alt	Controversial, sexual, and unusual topics; not always carried by servers.
biz	Business.
comp	Computers and related subjects.
humanities	Fine art, literature and philosophy.
misc	Discussions that don't fit anywhere else.
news	News about Usenet and its groups.
rec	Hobbies, games and recreation.
sci	Applied science, social science and engineering.
soc	Social groups, often ethnically related.
talk	Politics, current issues and debate.

With such an almost unlimited choice, you should very soon be able to subscribe to your own unique reading list of newsgroups. Subscribing does not mean you have to pay something, but means that when you enter News you will only see the groups in which you are most interested, and won't have to search through all of the others every time.

Starting to Read News

Initially you can start the News process from the opening window of Outlook Express 6, by clicking the **Set up a Newsgroups account** link as shown below.

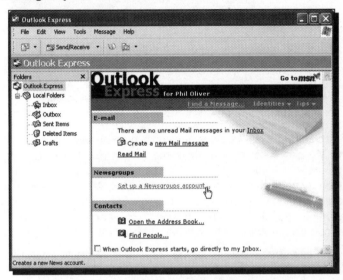

Fig. 9.1 The Outlook Express Default Opening Page

When first used, this opens the Internet Connection Wizard for you to complete your details. Once this has been done and you have subscribed to one, or more, newsgroups, you simply click on one of the newsgroup folders that are added to the Folders List to access it.

Internet News Configuration

Before you can access the Usenet groups you must make sure that your details and those of your news server are entered into the Internet Connection Wizard. If necessary, you can open this from the **Tools**, **Accounts**, **News** settings box by clicking the **Add** button and then selecting **News**. Complete the details in the dialogue boxes as they are presented, entering the server name in the **News (NNTP) server** field, as shown in Fig. 9.2 on the next page.

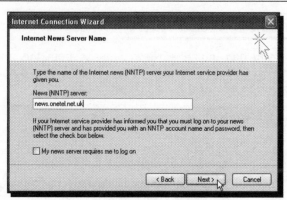

Fig. 9.2 Entering the News Server Details

If this is a closed, or members-only type server, then select the **My news server requires me to log on** check box and complete the log-on details which you should have been given by your ISP. Otherwise complete the Wizard boxes and keep clicking **Next** until finally the program starts downloading the server groups. Be warned the whole procedure can take well over half an hour.

As can be seen in some of our examples, we use Onetel.net as one of our Internet Service Providers. Their News service seems to be available to anyone that registers, so you should have no problem following our examples if you want to. Their News service has about 35,000 newsgroups, which is nowhere near complete. To get 'all' of the 80,000 plus groups, especially some of the more exciting 'alt' ones, you would probably have to register with one of the other more expensive pay services.

There are also hundreds of open news servers on the Internet that allow you to connect to them without a password. You should be able to find lists of them by searching for 'open news servers' with one of the search engines. When we tried it with Google there were about a hundred to explore, but remember that open news servers do not often stay permanently available.

The Newsgroup Subscriptions Window

The initial set-up procedure finishes by downloading a list of all the groups available on the news server. As there are well over 35,000 available to some servers this can take quite a while. When this is done, a window similar to ours below opens and you can see what newsgroups are available to you. If you are subscribed to more than one server, the **Newsgroup** pane lists the groups available from the server selected in the **Account(s)** pane.

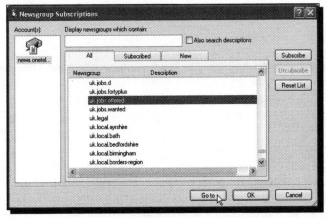

Fig. 9.3 The Newsgroup Subscriptions Dialogue Box

If you scroll down through the list of groups, almost at the bottom you should find some that start with **uk**. In our example, we selected **uk.jobs.offered** and clicked the **Go to** button, which is an easy way to have a look at the contents of a group.

An easier way would have been to type 'uk.jobs' into the **Display newsgroups which contain** field. Only the ones that matched this criterion would then have displayed.

A one-line header (for each of the first 300 of the 1,021 messages contained in the group that day), was loaded into the Message Header pane, as shown in Fig. 9.4. Still not too much unemployment in the computer industry these days!

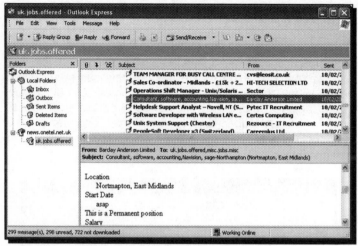

Fig. 9.4 The Outlook Express News Window

As soon as one of these headers is selected, the message itself appears in the Preview pane below it. This can take a few moments, don't forget it has to be downloaded over the network from your server.

Subscribing to a Group

If you think a group looks interesting and would be useful in the future, you should subscribe to it. To do this, re-open the Newsgroup Subscriptions window by clicking the Newsgroups Toolbar button, highlight the group and click the **Subscribe** button. A subscribe icon 🐝 is placed alongside the group name in the listing. To remove a group from your subscribed list, you simply select it and click the **Unsubscribe** button.

Once you have selected all the groups you regularly want to keep tabs on, click the **Subscribed** tab button at the top of the list. In the future, each time you open the Newsgroups window, it will only display your chosen list. At any time while this window is open you can click **All** to see a complete listing again, or **New** to see any new groups.

The News Window

The News window, shown in Fig. 9.4, is almost the same as the Main e-mail window. It contains three panes, a Folders List, a Message Header List, and a Preview pane.

Clicking on a Newsgroup in the Folders List, displays a listing of that group's current headers in the Message Header List, which by default has seven columns:

	Message has file(s) attached.
	Message is marked for offline viewing.
	Watch/ignore this conversation.
Subject	Shows the subject line of the message.
From	Gives the 'name' of the sender of the news message.
Sent	States the date and time the message was posted to the group.
Size	Gives the size of the file in KB.

You can sort messages by any of these columns and in ascending or descending order, by clicking in the column header. You can also add, remove, hide or rearrange the columns, and sort them, in the Columns box, shown in Fig. 9.5, opened with the **View**, **Columns** menu command.

Clicking on a message header, when you are on-line, downloads and displays the message body text in the Preview pane.

Fig. 9.5 Setting Columns

The News Toolbar

Opens a New Message window for creating a new posting, with the To: field blank.

Opens the New Message window for sending a message to be posted in the currently selected newsgroup.

Opens the New Message window for replying privately to the sender of the current news message, with the To: field pre-addressed to the original sender.

Opens the New Message window for forwarding the current news message. The To: field is blank. The original Subject field is prefixed with Fw:.

Prints the current message.

Stops the current downloading operation. This option is only available when the download Status Indicator in the top right corner of the window is rotating.

Attempts to make a dial-up connection and downloads selected messages or headers, as well as updating any e-mail folders and sending any waiting messages.

Opens the Outlook Express Address Book.

Lets you search for messages, text, or for people's e-mail details.

Opens the Newsgroup Subscriptions window in which you select which news server to use and the groups subscribed to.

Downloads new headers for the selected group from the server, in batches of 300.

The Read Message Window

Double-clicking on a message header in the News window, opens a Read Message window with the message in it, as shown in Fig. 9.6 below.

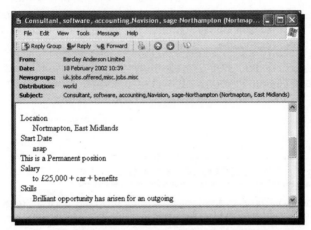

Fig. 9.6 The Outlook Express Read Message Window

This window has its own menu and Toolbar, and moving the mouse pointer over a Toolbar button shows what the button's action will be. Apart from the three icons described next, this window is very much the same as the e-mail Read Message window described in an earlier chapter.

Replying to Messages

As long as you have chosen to make Outlook Express your default news reader in the **Tools**, **Options**, **General** settings box, the News window Toolbar icons will use Outlook Express's Mail facilities to easily send messages of three different types.

The **Reply to Group** icon addresses your message to the current newsgroup for all to read.

The **Reply to Sender** icon addresses an e-mail message to the individual who posted the current news message.

The **Forward** icon prepares an e-mail with a copy of the current message, for you to address and complete.

Be very careful not to mix these up, the result could be embarrassing if you post a very personal message to the whole group, for maybe millions of people to read!

Postings Containing Pictures

If you have time to explore the many thousands of **alt** groups, you will find that a lot of them contain messages with picture files attached that are (or should be) relevant to the group name. Our example in Fig. 9.7 below shows one being downloaded from a group that does not normally need censoring, but be warned, many of them do! You never really know what you will find in them.

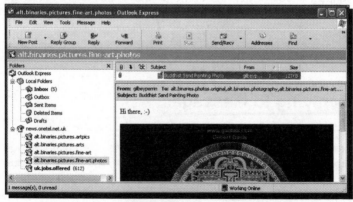

Fig. 9.7 A Graphic Image Showing in the Preview Pane

Clicking a message in the Header Pane will, as long as you are connected, download the message body in the Preview pane, and you will be able to view any graphics in the message, as shown in Fig. 9.7. When the image file has been completely downloaded, you can right-click the picture and use the **Save Picture As** command to save it to your hard disc.

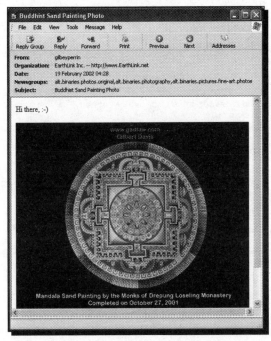

Fig. 9.8 A Graphic Image Showing in the Preview Pane

The same message with its art graphic is shown in Fig 9.8 above, but this time opened in its own Read Message window, by double-clicking the message header.

Attachments are usually shown with a paperclip icon on the message title bar. When this is the case, to save a file attachment, use the **File**, **Save Attachments** menu command, or right-click the attachment and select the **Save Picture As** option.

Threaded Messages

When a message is placed on a newsgroup, often someone replies and then a 'thread' or 'conversation' is formed.

News message icons

The following icons indicate whether a conversation (a topic and all of its responses) is expanded or collapsed, and whether messages and headers are marked as read or unread.

This icon	Indicates this
⊞	This level of the conversation is collapsed. Click the icon to show all the responses (expand the conversation).
⊟	This level of the conversation is expanded. Click the icon to hide all the responses (collapse the conversation).
🗍	The message has not been not opened. The heading appears in bold type.
🗍	The message header has been marked read.
🗎	The message has been marked read, and is stored in a message file on your computer.
🗎	The message has not been marked as read, and the header and body are stored in a message file on your computer.
🗎	The message is no longer available on the server.
↓	The news message is marked to be downloaded.
⊞↓	The news message and all conversations are marked to be downloaded.
⊟↓	The individual news message (without conversations) is marked to be downloaded.
🗎	The news message has been replied to.
🗎	The news message has been forwarded.
✳	The newsgroup is new on the server.
🗎	The message is in progress in the Drafts folder.
⚑	The message is flagged.
👓	The conversation is watched.
⊘	The conversation is ignored.

Fig. 9.9 News Message Status Icons

The edited News Help window in Fig. 9.9 above shows how you can recognise the status of any news messages in the Message Header list of a News window. Outlook Express messages are not threaded by default, but you can change this by checking the **Automatically expand grouped**

messages option in the **Tools**, **Options**, **Read** settings sheet. Message replies would then always be placed with the original messages.

If you want the message list to display only the original message in a thread (conversation), select the first message, and then use the **View**, **Collapse** menu command, or click the minus (-) sign next to the original message.

Offline Viewing

If, like most of us, you are usually busy and don't have time to wait for long newsgroup messages to be downloaded, you can synchronise your accounts, or set up a batch download process, and view selected headers or whole messages off-line later on.

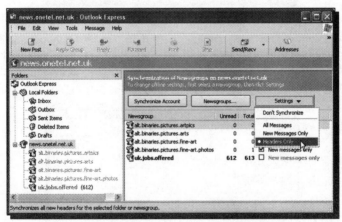

Fig. 9.10 Using the Synchronize Settings Button

In the Main window in Offline mode, select one or more newsgroups you subscribe to whose messages you want to read offline. Click the **Settings** button, and then select the option you want from the drop-down menu, as in Fig. 9.10 shown above. This marks what you want transferred from the server to your computer during synchronisation.

All Messages	Download all messages on the server to your computer.
New Messages Only	Download only messages that are new to the server since you last synchronised.
Headers Only	Download only headers with details of message subject, author, date, and size.

Whenever you want to transfer the messages or headers to your computer from the server, click the **Synchronize Account** button and go and make a cup of coffee.

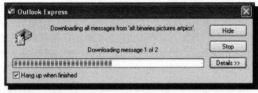

Fig. 9.11 The Brief Downloading Status Message Box

A downloading box, similar to that in Fig. 9.11 above, will show you how the download process is going. You can click the **Details** button to see more information about what is happening, as shown in Fig. 9.12 below.

Fig. 9.12 The Detailed Downloading Status Message Box

If you are using a modem connection, you should definitely check the **Hang up when finished** option. Your phone bill will almost certainly be big enough already!

After you download messages for off-line reading and have disconnected from the Internet, you can return to the News Window and the message header icons, shown in Fig. 9.9, will show the status of any saved, or cached, headers or messages. Clicking the **View**, **Current View**, **Show Downloaded Messages** menu command, will display only the downloaded messages for you to read. Have fun.

Newsgroup Caches

Each newsgroup you subscribe to has its own cache file on your computer and everything you download from that group, either manually or for off-line viewing, is saved in this cache. When you select to view an item that is stored in a cache it is 'instantly' displayed, as it does not have to be downloaded. This is all very well, but if you are not careful you can fill your hard disc up with material you don't even know you are keeping.

Controlling the Caches

The **Tools**, **Options**, **Maintenance** settings sheet gives you control of the size of all your cached message files when you click the **Clean Up Now** button as shown in Fig. 9.13 at the top of the next page.

This opens the Local File Clean Up box shown in Fig. 9.14 in which you can manually compact, delete, or remove messages from all or specific message files, newsgroups, or servers.

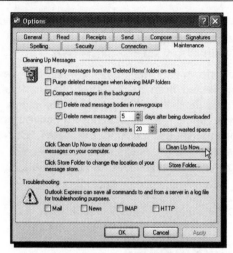

Fig. 9.13 The Cleaning Up Messages Options

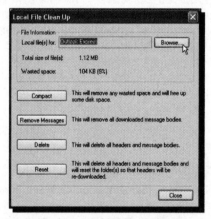

Fig. 9.14 The Local File Clean Up Box

You access all these 'local' files on your PC by clicking the **Browse** button and selecting the server or newsgroups you want to work with, as shown in Fig. 9.15.

This clean-up procedure is usually known as 'purging'. Some of these 'manual clean up' options are also available from the News menu with the **File**, **Folder** command.

Fig. 9.15 Cleaning Up an Individual Newsgroup

Purging unused, old, or large newsgroups can increase your free hard disc space enormously. Most news servers remove old messages and headers on a regular basis, sometimes even weekly. The next time you connect to a newsgroup you've purged, your cache is rebuilt with just the current messages and headers from the server.

On Your Own

You should, by now, have enough basic knowledge to happily venture forth into the unknown.

Good luck, but please remember that there are millions of other newsgroup readers, and you never know where, or who, they are. Please watch what you say, or include, in your postings, there is enough rubbish there already.

One problem we have had after using one of our main e-mail addresses in news postings, was an enormous and growing amount of 'junk mail' to that address. To avoid this we strongly recommend that you set up a Hotmail account (page 130) to use specially for your interactive news sessions. Hotmail is quite good at dealing with junk mail, and as a last resort you can just abandon the account and open another one.

10

Behaviour on the Internet

As we saw in the first chapter, the Internet has grown up without any real control. It has grown, just like Topsy, but some of the behaviour you see there is not always quite as nice. We will not talk about pornography, or worse. If that is what you want, it is almost certainly there to be found (as in most major cities of the world), but increasingly most of it is hidden behind closed doors. Most really dubious Web sites require membership and payment, but the Usenet groups are still a problem. If you have children that use your computer to surf the Web, Internet Explorer has a security feature to help enable you to control what they are exposed to, this is briefly discussed at the end of the chapter.

We will very briefly mention some of the more dubious behaviour patterns you may encounter on your way round the Internet, especially in the newsgroups, and to a lesser extent the mailing lists.

Internet Flames

A flame is a particularly nasty, personal attack on somebody for something he, or she, has written in a posting. Newsgroups are notorious for flaming (burning people up). This can sometimes lead to long and drawn-out discussions on what really are stupid matters. These 'flame wars' can sometimes be fun to watch at first, but quickly grow boring, and become a general waste of everyone's time and mail space.

But, be warned, if you start posting to groups you may well upset someone, without even meaning to. If they are vicious, you may get flamed.

Spam, Spam, Bacon and Spam

Spamming, on the Internet, is the practice of sending a message to a very large number of people, newsgroups and mailing lists. It is named after the Monty Python sketch, where you could have what you liked in the restaurant as long as it had Spam with it. A spammer gives you little choice, you have to download his posting, but you don't have to read it.

It will not be long before you encounter this 'problem' in some form, or other. Often a product, service, chain letter or a get rich quick scheme is being offered. We tend to ignore them and hope they will go away.

Other Usenet Types

There are a number of other Usenet types you'll soon come to recognise, and love:

- Ones that think their topic of interest should be forced on everyone else as frequently as possible. Often posting dozens of messages to unrelated groups, sometimes with ethnic contents.

- Ones that take pages of message to get nowhere. This often includes excessive quoting by including the entire message in their reply, rather than deleting the irrelevant portions.

- Ones who enjoy insulting others and post nasty, or even obscene, messages in unrelated newsgroups.

- Ones who include enormous signatures at the end of their postings, often including enormous text graphics. These are harmless, but can be annoying, and they take longer to download.

Some Internet Etiquette

Often called 'netiquette' the following list, we once found[1], although somewhat stilted makes good reading and should help you avoid upsetting too many people on the Net:

1   DON'T include the entire contents of a previous posting in your reply.

DO cut mercilessly. Leave just enough to indicate what you're responding to. NEVER include mail headers except maybe the 'From:' line. If you can't figure out how to delete lines in your mailer software, paraphrase or re-type the quoted material.

2   DON'T reply to a point in a message without quoting or paraphrasing what you're responding to.

DO quote (briefly) or paraphrase. If the original 'Subject:' line was 'Big dogs' make sure yours says 'Re: Big dogs'. Some REPLY functions do this automatically. By net convention, included lines are preceded by '>' (greater-than signs).

3   DON'T send lines longer than 70 characters. This is a kindness to folks with terminal-based mail editors. Some mail gateways truncate extra characters turning your deathless prose into gibberish.

Some mail editor tools only SEEM to insert line breaks for you, but actually don't, so that every paragraph is one immense line. Learn what your mail editor does.

4   DON'T SEND A MESSAGE IN ALL CAPS. CAPITALISED MESSAGES ARE HARDER TO READ THAN LOWER CASE OR MIXED CASE.

---

[1]   Patrick Crispen's Internet Roadmap

DO use normal capitalisation. Separate your paragraphs with blank lines. Make your message inviting to your potential readers.

5   DON'T betray confidences. It is all too easy to quote a personal message and regret it.

DO read the 'To:' and 'Cc:' lines in your message before you send it. Are you SURE you want the mail to go there?

6   DON'T make statements which can be interpreted as official positions of your organisation, or of offers to do business.

DO treat every post as though you were sending a copy to your boss, your minister, and your worst enemy.

7   DON'T rely on the ability of your readers to tell the difference between serious statements and satire, or sarcasm. It's hard to write funny. It's even harder to write satire.

DO remember that no one can hear your tone of voice. You can use smileys, like:

:-) or **:->**

turn your head anti-clockwise to see the smile.

You can also use capitals for emphasis, or use Net conventions for italics and underlines as in: "You said the guitar solo on "Comfortably Numb" from Pink Floyd's, The Wall, was *lame*? Are you OUT OF YOUR MIND???!!!"

8   DON'T send a message that says nothing but "Me, too", or something equally as trivial. This is most annoying when combined with (1) or (2) above.

Censoring your Web Browser

Internet Explorer 6 allows you to control what Web sites your children can access. This feature is located on the **Tools**, **Internet Options**, **Content** settings sheet shown in Fig. 10.1.

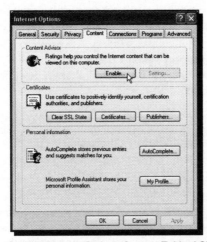

Fig. 10.1 The Internet Options Content Tabbed Sheet

Fig. 10.2 The Content Advisor

Clicking the **Enable** button opens the Content Adviser control window, shown in Fig. 10.2 on the previous page.

This has four sliders to allow you to set the degree of language, nudity, sex and violence you want your children (or other users) to be exposed to. This facility depends on Web sites having a rating system 'attached to them'.

The Content Adviser then filters out unsuitable sites and prohibits access to them. The site rating service is provided by the Internet Content Rating Association (ICRA). Their labelling system has replaced the RSACi system but works in a similar way, and is backwards compatible!

To become rated, Web authors fill in an online questionnaire; this generates a label which they add to their site. ICRA labels are invisible to site visitors and are objective descriptions of the content of the site. Value judgements can then be made by the users. There is the facility to select others in the **Advanced** tab section of the Content Advisor.

By default, if a Web site does not have a rating your users will not be able to access it. They will be presented with a blacked out screen if they try. You can alter this, however, in

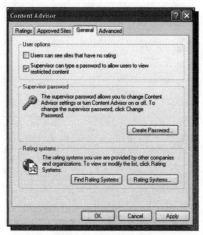

Fig. 10.3 The Content Advisor General Section

the **General** tab section shown in Fig. 10.3, by checking the **Users can see sites that have no rating** option. Also in this section you can use the **Change Password** feature.

When you have made all the settings you want, press **OK** enough times to close the Content Adviser. You will be asked to establish a password, but please don't forget it or you will find yourself re-installing Explorer in the future! You have now censored your computer, probably for the first time!

To cancel, or change, your security settings in the future, open the **Tools**, **Internet Options**, **Content** sheet and click the **Disable** button. You will need your password to access the Content Adviser.

This measure could also be usefully used by organisations to limit their personnel to specific sites on the Internet. This would not be a popular measure, but would almost certainly reduce the amount of wasted time.

Still a Feature for the Future

We feel this feature is a commendable attempt by Microsoft, Netscape and the 'establishment' to make surfing the Web a safer place for your children, but it does depend on all the 'non-exotic' sites getting rated. At the moment this is anything but the case.

11

Glossary of Terms

Access control   A security mechanism that
                 determines which operations a user is
                 authorised to perform on a PC, a file,
                 a printer, etc.

Active   Describes the folder, window or icon
                 that you are currently using or that is
                 currently selected.

Active partition A partition from which an x86-based
                 computer starts up. The active
                 partition must be a primary partition
                 on a basic disc.

ActiveX   A set of technologies that allows
                 software components to interact with
                 one another in a networked
                 environment, regardless of the
                 language in which the components
                 were created.

Add-in   A mini-program which runs in
                 conjunction with another and
                 enhances its functionality.

Address   A unique number or name that
                 identifies a specific computer or user
                 on a network.

Administrator   For Windows XP Professional, a
                 person responsible for setting up and
                 managing local computers, their user
                 and group accounts, and assigning
                 passwords and permissions.

Anonymous FTP	Anonymous FTP allows you to connect to a remote computer and transfer public files back to your local computer without the need to have a user ID and password.
Applet	A small Java program that can be downloaded over a network and launched on the user's computer.
Application	Software (program) designed to carry out a certain activity, such as word processing, or data management.
Archie	Archie is an Internet service that allows you to locate files that can be downloaded via FTP.
ARPANet	Advanced Research Projects Agency Network. The precursor to the Internet.
ASCII	A binary code representation of a character set. The name stands for 'American Standard Code for Information Interchange'.
ASP	Active Server Page. File format used for dynamic Web pages that get their data from a server based database.
Association	An identification of a filename extension to a program. This lets Windows open the program when its files are selected.
Audio input device	A device that records music and voice input into your computer, such as a microphone or a CD-ROM player.
Authentication	The process for verifying that an entity or object is who or what it claims to be.

Authoring	The process of creating web documents or software.
AVI	Audio Video Interleaved. A Windows multimedia file format for sound and moving pictures.
Backbone	The main transmission lines of the Internet, running at over 45 Mbps.
Background	The screen background image used on a graphical user interface such as Windows.
Backup	To make a back-up copy of a file or a disc for safekeeping.
Bandwidth	The range of transmission frequencies a network can use. The greater the bandwidth the more information that can be transferred over a network.
Banner	An advertising graphic shown on a Web page.
BASIC	Beginner's All-purpose Symbolic Instruction Code - a high-level programming language.
Basic volume	A primary partition or logical drive that resides on a basic disc.
Batch file	A file that contains commands which are automatically executed when the file is run.
Baud rate	The speed at which a modem communicates.
BBS	Bulletin Board System, a computer equipped with software and telecoms links that acts as an information host for remote computer systems.

Beta test	A test of software that is still under development, by people actually using the software.
Binary	A base-2 number system in which values are expressed as combinations of two digits, 0 and 1.
BIOS	On x86-based computers, the set of software routines that test hardware at startup, start the operating system, and support the transfer of data among hardware devices.
Bit	The smallest unit of information handled by a computer.
Bitmap	A technique for managing the image displayed on a computer screen.
Bookmark	A marker inserted at a specific point in a document to which the user may wish to return for later reference.
Boot partition	The partition on a hard disc that contains the operating system and its support files.
Boot up	To start your computer by switching it on, which initiates a self test of its Random Access Memory (RAM), then loads the necessary system files.
bps	Bits-Per-Second. Speed that data is moved from one place to another. A 56K modem can move about 57,000 bits per second.
Broadband	A communications systems in which the medium of transmission (such as a wire or fibre-optic cable) carries multiple messages at a time.

Broadcast	An address that is destined for all hosts on a particular network segment.
Browse	A button in some Windows dialogue boxes that lets you view a list of files and folders before you make a selection. Also to view Internet Web pages online.
Browser	A program, like the Internet Explorer, that lets you view Web pages.
Bug	An error in coding or logic that causes a program to malfunction.
Bus	A communication line used for data transfer among the components of a computer system.
Button	A graphic element in a dialogue box or toolbar that performs a specified function.
Byte	A unit of data that holds a single character, such as a letter, a digit.
Cable modem	A device that enables a broadband connection to the Internet by using cable television infrastructure.
Cache	An area of memory, or disc space, reserved for data, which speeds up downloading.
Card	A removable printed-circuit board that is plugged into a computer expansion slot.
CD-R	Recordable compact disc.
CD-ROM	Read Only Memory compact disc. Data can be read but not written.

CD-RW	Rewritable compact disc. Data can be copied to the CD on more than one occasion and can be erased.
CGI	Common Gateway Interface - a convention for servers to communicate with local applications and allow users to provide information to scripts attached to web pages, usually through forms.
Cgi-bin	The most common name of a directory on a web server in which CGI programs are stored.
Chart	A graphical view of data that is used to visually display trends, patterns, and comparisons.
Click	To press and release a mouse button once without moving the mouse.
Client	A computer that has access to services over a computer network. The computer providing the services is a server.
Client application	A Windows application that can accept linked, or embedded, objects.
Clipboard	A temporary storage area of memory, where text and graphics are stored with the Windows cut and copy actions.
Cluster	In data storage, the smallest amount of disc space that can be allocated to hold a file.
Code page	A means of providing support for character sets and keyboard layouts for different countries or regions.
Command	An instruction given to a computer to carry out a particular action.

Command prompt	A window used to interface with the MS-DOS operating system.
Compressed file	One that is compacted to save server space and reduce transfer times. Typical file extensions for compressed files include .zip (DOS/-Windows) and .tar (UNIX).
Configuration	A general purpose term referring to the way you have your computer set up.
Controls	Objects on a form, report, or data access page that display data, perform actions, or are used for decoration.
Cookies	Files sent by a Web server and stored on your hard drive by your browser that hold information for it to send to the server the next time it is accessed.
CPU	The Central Processing Unit; the main chip that executes all instructions entered into a computer.
Cyberspace	Originated by William Gibson in his novel 'Neuromancer', now used to describe the Internet and the other computer networks.
Data access page	A Web page, created by Access, that has a connection to a database; you can view, add, edit, and manipulate the data in this page.
Data packet	A unit of information transmitted as a whole from one device to another on a network.
Database	A collection of data related to a particular topic or purpose.

DBMS	Database management system - A software interface between the database and the user.
Default	The command, device or option automatically chosen.
Defragmentation	The process of rewriting parts of a file to contiguous sectors on a hard disc to increase the speed of access and retrieval.
Desktop	The Windows screen working background, on which you place icons, folders, etc.
Device driver	A special file that must be loaded into memory for Windows to be able to address a specific procedure or hardware device.
Device name	A logical name used by DOS to identify a device, such as LPT1 or COM1 for the parallel or serial printer.
Dial-up connection	The connection to a network via a device that uses the telephone network. This includes modems with a standard phone line, ISDN cards with high-speed ISDN lines, or X.25 networks.
Dialogue box	A window displayed on the screen to allow the user to enter information.
Digital signature	A means for originators of a message, file, or other digitally encoded information to bind their identity to the information.
Direct Connection	A permanent connection between your computer system and the Internet.

Directory	An area on disc where information relating to a group of files is kept. Also known as a folder.
Disconnect	To detach a drive, port or computer from a shared device, or to break an Internet connection.
Display adapter	An expansion board that plugs into a PC to give it display capabilities.
DLL	Dynamic Link Library; An OS feature that allows files with the .dll extensions to be loaded only when needed by the program.
Document	A file produced by an application program. When used in reference to the Web, a document is any file containing text, media or hyperlinks that can be transferred from an HTTP server to a browser.
Domain	A group of devices, servers and computers on a network.
Domain Name	The unique name of an Internet site, for example www.microsoft.com, which allows you to reference them without knowing their true numerical address.
DOS	Disc Operating System. A collection of small specialised programs that allow interaction between user and computer.
Double-click	To quickly press and release a mouse button twice.
Download	To transfer to your computer a file, or data, from another computer.
DPI	Dots Per Inch - a resolution standard for laser printers.

Drag	To move an object on the screen by pressing and holding down the left mouse button while moving the mouse.
Drive name	The letter followed by a colon which identifies a floppy or hard disc drive.
DSL	Digital Subscriber Line - a broad-band connection to the Internet through existing copper telephone wires.
Dual boot	A PC configuration that can start two different operating systems.
DVD	Digital Versatile Disc; a type of optical disc technology. It looks like a CD but can store greater amounts of data.
EISA	Extended Industry Standard Architecture, for construction of PCs with the Intel 32-bit microprocessor.
E-mail	Electronic Mail - A system that allows computer users to send and receive messages electronically.
Embedded object	Information in a document that is 'copied' from its source application. Selecting the object opens the creating application from within the document.
Encrypted password	A password that is scrambled.
Engine	Software used by search services.
Ethernet	A very common method of networking computers in a LAN.
Expansion slot	A socket in a computer, designed to hold expansion boards and connect them to the system bus.
Extract a file	Create an uncompressed copy of the file in a folder you specify.

FAQ	Frequently Asked Questions - A common feature on the Internet, FAQs are files of answers to commonly asked questions.
FAT	The File Allocation Table. An area on disc where information is kept on which part of the disc a file is located.
File extension	The suffix following the period in a filename. Windows uses this to identify the source application program. For example .mdb indicates an Access file.
Filename	The name given to a file. In Windows 95 and above this can be up to 256 characters long.
Filter	A set of criteria that is applied to data to show a subset of the data.
Finger	An Internet software tool for locating people on other Internet sites.
Firewall	Security measures designed to protect a networked system from unauthorised access.
Floppy disc	A removable disc on which information can be stored magnetically.
Folder	An area used to store a group of files, usually with a common link.
Font	A graphic design representing a set of characters, numbers and symbols.
Format	The structure of a file that defines the way it is stored and laid out on the screen or in print.
Fragmentation	The scattering of parts of the same file over different areas of the disc.

Free space	Available disc space that can be used to create logical drives within an extended partition.
Freeware	Software that is available for downloading and unlimited use without charge.
FTP	File Transfer Protocol. The procedure for connecting to a remote computer and transferring files.
Function key	One of the series of 10 or 12 keys marked with the letter F and a numeral, used for specific operations.
Gateway	A computer system that allows otherwise incompatible networks to communicate with each other.
GIF	Graphics Interchange Format, a common standard for images on the Web.
Gigabyte	(GB); 1,024 Megabytes. Usually thought of as one billion bytes.
Gopher	Invented just before the Web, gopher was a widely successful method of making menus of material available over the Internet.
Graphic	A picture or illustration, also called an image. Formats include GIF, JPEG, BMP, PCX, and TIFF.
Graphics card	A device that controls the display on the monitor and other allied functions.
Group	A collection of users, computers, contacts, and other groups.
GUI	A Graphic User Interface, such as Windows, the software front-end

	meant to provide an attractive and easy to use interface.
Handshaking	A series of signals acknowledging that communication can take place between computers or other devices.
Hard copy	Output on paper.
Hard disc	A device built into the computer for holding programs and data.
Hardware	The equipment that makes up a computer system, excluding the programs or software.
Help	A Windows system that gives you instructions and additional information on using a program.
Helper application	A program allowing you to view multimedia files that your web browser cannot handle internally.
Hibernation	A state in which your computer shuts down after saving everything in memory on your hard disc.
Hit	A single request from a web browser for a single item from a web server.
Home page	The document displayed when you first open your Web browser, or the first document you come to at a Web site.
Host	Computer connected directly to the Internet that provides services to other local and/or remote computers.
Hotlist	A list of frequently used Web locations and URL addresses.
HTML	HyperText Markup Language, the format used in most documents on the Web.

HTML editor	Authoring tool which assists with the creation of HTML pages.
HTTP	HyperText Transport Protocol, the system used to link and transfer hypertext documents on the Web.
Hub	A common connection point for devices in a network.
Hyperlink	A segment of text, or an image, that refers to another document on the Web, an intranet or your PC.
Hypermedia	Hypertext extended to include linked multimedia.
Hypertext	A system that allows documents to be cross-linked so that the reader can explore related links, or documents, by clicking on a highlighted symbol.
Icon	A small graphic image that represents a function or object. Clicking on an icon produces an action.
ICS	Internet Connection Sharing.
Image	See graphic.
IMAP	Internet Message Access Protocol. IMAP is gradually replacing POP as the main protocol used by e-mail clients in communicating with e-mail servers.
Insertion point	A flashing bar that shows where typed text will be entered into a document.
Interface	A device that allows you to connect a computer to its peripherals.
Internet	The global system of computer networks.

Intranet	A private network inside an organisation using the same kind of software as the Internet.
IP	Internet Protocol - The rules that provide basic Internet functions.
IP Address	Internet Protocol Address - every computer on the Internet has a unique identifying number.
IRC	Internet Relay Chat. A large multi-user live 'chat' facility. There are a number of major IRC servers around the world which are linked to each other. Anyone can create a channel and anything that anyone types in a given channel is seen by all others in the channel.
ISA	Industry Standard Architecture; a standard for internal PC connections.
ISDN	Integrated Services Digital Network; a telecom standard using digital transmission technology to support voice, video and data communications applications over regular telephone lines.
ISP	Internet Service Provider - A company that offers access to the Internet.
Java	An object-oriented programming language created by Sun Micro-systems for developing applications and applets that are capable of running on any computer, regardless of the operating system.
JavaScript	A programming language mostly used in Web pages, usually to add features that make the page interactive.

JPEG / JPG	Joint Photographic Experts Group, a popular cross-platform format for image files. JPEG is best suited for true colour original images.
Kernel	The core of layered architecture that manages the most basic operations of the operating system and the computer's processor.
Kilobyte	(KB); 1024 bytes of information or storage space.
LAN	Local Area Network - High-speed, privately-owned network covering a limited geographical area, such as an office or a building.
Laptop	A portable computer small enough to sit on your lap.
LCD	Liquid Crystal Display.
Linked object	An object that is inserted into a document but still exists in the source file. Changing the original object automatically updates it within the linked document.
Links	The hypertext connections between Web pages.
Linux	A version of the UNIX operating system for PCs which incorporates a Graphical User Interface (GUI) similar to that of Microsoft Windows.
Local	A resource that is located on your computer, not linked to it over a network.
Location	An Internet address.
Log on	To gain access to a network.

Maillist	An automated system that allows people to send e-mail to one address, where it is copied and sent to all the subscribers to the list.
MBR	The first sector on a hard disc, which starts the process of booting the computer.
MCI	Media Control Interface - a standard for files and multimedia devices.
Megabyte	(MB); 1024 kilobytes of information or storage space.
Megahertz	(MHz); Speed of processor in millions of cycles per second.
Memory	Part of computer consisting of storage elements organised into addressable locations that can hold data and instructions.
Menu	A list of available options in an application.
Menu bar	The horizontal bar that lists the names of menus.
MIDI	Musical Instrument Digital Interface - enables devices to transmit and receive sound and music messages.
MIME	Multipurpose Internet Mail Extensions, a messaging standard that allows Internet users to exchange e-mail messages enhanced with graphics, video and voice.
MIPS	Million Instructions Per Second; measures speed of a system.
Mirror site	A Web, or FTP, site that maintains copies of material originated at another location, to provide more

widespread and faster access to the resource.

Modem   Short for Modulator-demodulator. An electronic device that lets computers communicate electronically.

Monitor   The display device connected to your PC, also called a screen.

Mouse   A device used to manipulate a pointer around your display and activate processes by pressing buttons.

MPEG   Motion Picture Experts Group - a video file format offering excellent quality in a relatively small file.

MS-DOS   Microsoft's implementation of the Disc Operating System for PCs.

Multimedia   The use of photographs, music and sound and movie images in a presentation.

Multitasking   Performing more than one operation at the same time.

My Documents   A folder that provides a convenient place to store documents, graphics, or other files you want to access quickly.

Netiquette   The etiquette on the Internet.

Network   Two or more computers connected together to share resources.

Network adapter   A device that connects your computer to a network.

Network server   Central computer which stores files for several linked computers.

Newsgroup   The name for discussion groups on Usenet.

Node	Any single computer connected to a network.
NTFS file system	An advanced file system that provides performance, security, reliability, and advanced features that are not found in any version of FAT.
ODBC	Open DataBase Connectivity - A standard protocol for accessing information in a SQL database server.
OLE	Object Linking and Embedding - A technology for transferring and sharing information among software applications.
Online	Having access to the Internet.
On-line Service	Services such as America On-line and CompuServe that provide content to subscribers and usually connections to the Internet.
Operating system	Software that runs a computer.
Page	An HTML document, or Web site.
Parallel port	The input/output connector for a parallel interface device. Printers are generally plugged into a parallel port.
Partition	A portion of a physical disc that functions as though it were a physically separate disc.
Password	A unique character string used to gain access to a network, program, or mailbox.
PATH	The location of a file in the directory tree.

PCI	Peripheral Component Interconnect - a type of slot in your computer which accepts similar type peripheral cards.
Peripheral	Any device attached to a PC.
Perl	A popular language for programming CGI applications.
PIF file	Program information file - gives information to Windows about an MS-DOS application.
Pixel	A picture element on screen; the smallest element that can be independently assigned colour and intensity.
Plug-and-play	Hardware which can be plugged into a PC and be used immediately without configuration.
Plug-in	Software that adds features to a Web browser and server.
POP	Post Office Protocol - a method of storing and returning e-mail.
Port	The place where information goes into or out of a computer, e.g. a modem might be connected to the serial port.
Portal	A Web site that is set up to be the first place people see when using the Web. Portals have links to other web sites and usually a search engine. In fact any services to attract people to use that site as their main point of entry to the Web.
Posting	A single message entered into a network communications system.
Posix	The specification for a look-alike UNIX operating system drawn up by

	the American National Standards Institute (ANSI). Linux is an independent Posix implementation.
PostScript	A page-description language (PDL), developed by Adobe Systems for printing on laser printers.
PPP	Point-to-Point Protocol - One of two methods (see SLIP) for using special software to establish a temporary direct connection to the Internet over regular phone lines.
Print queue	A list of print jobs waiting to be sent to a printer.
Program	A set of instructions which cause a computer to perform tasks.
Protocol	A set of rules or standards that define how computers communicate with each other.
Query	The set of keywords and operators sent by a user to a search engine, or a database search request.
Queue	A list of e-mail messages waiting to be sent over the Internet.
RAM	Random Access Memory. The computer's volatile memory. Data held in it is lost when power is switched off.
Real mode	MS-DOS mode, typically used to run programs, such as MS-DOS games, that will not run under Windows.
Refresh	To update displayed information with current data.
Registered file type	File types that are tracked by the system registry and are recognised

by the programs you have installed on your computer.

Registry

A database where information about a computer's configuration is deposited. The registry contains information that Windows continually references during its operation.

Remote computer

A computer that you can access only by using a communications line or a communications device, such as a network card or a modem.

Resource

A directory, or printer, that can be shared over a network.

Robot

A Web agent that visits sites, by requesting documents from them, for the purposes of indexing for search engines. Also known as Wanderers, Crawlers, or Spiders.

ROM

Read Only Memory. A PC's non-volatile memory. Data is written into this memory at manufacture and is not affected by power loss.

Root

The highest or uppermost level in a hierarchically organised disc directory.

Screen saver

A moving picture or pattern that appears on your screen when you have not used the mouse or keyboard for a specified period of time.

Script

A type of program consisting of a set of instructions to an application or tool program.

Scroll bar

A bar that appears at the right side or bottom edge of a window.

Search

Submit a query to a search engine.

Search engine	A system that helps users find information across the Internet.
Serial interface	An interface that transfers data as individual bits.
Server	A computer system that manages and delivers information for client computers.
Shared resource	Any device, program or file that is available to network users.
Shareware	Software that is available on public networks and bulletin boards. Users are expected to pay a nominal amount to the software developer.
Shortcut	A link to any item accessible on your computer or on a network, such as a program, file, folder, disc drive, Web page, printer, or another computer.
Signature file	An ASCII text file, maintained within e-mail programs, that contains text for your signature.
Site	A place on the Internet. Every Web page has a location where it resides which is called its site.
SLIP	Serial Line Internet Protocol, a method of Internet connection that enables computers to use phone lines and a modem to connect to the Internet without having to connect to a host.
SMTP	Simple Mail Transfer Protocol - a protocol dictating how e-mail messages are exchanged over the Internet.
Socket	An endpoint for sending and receiving data between computers.

Software	The programs and instructions that control your PC.
Spamming	Sending the same message to a large number of mailing lists or newsgroups. Also to overload a Web page with excessive keywords in an attempt to get a better search ranking.
Spider	See robot.
Spooler	Software which handles transfer of information to a store to be used by a peripheral device.
SQL	Structured Query Language, used with relational databases.
SSL	Secure Sockets Layer, the standard transmission security protocol developed by Netscape, which has been put into the public domain.
Standby	A state in which your computer consumes less power when it is idle, but remains available for immediate use.
Subscribe	To become a member of.
Surfing	The process of looking around the Internet.
SVGA	Super Video Graphics Array; it has all the VGA modes but with 256, or more, colours.
Swap file	An area of your hard disc used to store temporary operating files, also known as virtual memory.
Sysop	System Operator - A person responsible for the physical

operations of a computer system or network resource.

System disc
A disc containing files to enable a PC to start up.

System files
Files used by Windows to load, configure, and run the operating system.

Task Manager
A utility that provides information about programs and processes running on the computer. Using Task Manager, you can end or run programs and end processes, and display a dynamic overview of your computer's performance.

TCP/IP
Transmission Control Protocol/ Internet Protocol, combined protocols that perform the transfer of data between two computers. TCP monitors and ensures the correct transfer of data. IP receives the data, breaks it up into packets, and sends it to a network within the Internet.

Telnet
A program which allows people to remotely use computers across networks.

Text file
An unformatted file of text characters saved in ASCII format.

Thread
An ongoing message-based conversation on a single subject.

TIFF
Tag Image File Format - a popular graphic image file format.

Toggle
To turn an action on and off with the same switch.

Tool
Software program used to support Web site creation and management.

Toolbar	A bar containing icons giving quick access to commands.
TrueType fonts	Fonts that can be scaled to any size and print as they show on the screen.
Uninstall	When referring to software, the act of removing program files and folders from your hard disc and removing related data from your registry so the software is no longer available.
UNIX	Multitasking, multi-user computer operating system that is run by many computer servers on networks.
Upload/Download	The process of transferring files between computers. Files are uploaded from your computer to another and downloaded from another computer to your own.
URL	Uniform Resource Locator, the addressing system used on the Web, containing information about the method of access, the server to be accessed and the path of the file to be accessed.
USB	Universal Serial Bus - an external bus standard that enables data transfer rates of 12 Mbps.
Usenet	Informal network of computers that allow the posting and reading of messages in newsgroups that focus on specific topics.
User ID	The unique identifier, usually used in conjunction with a password, which identifies you on a computer.
Virtual Reality	Simulations of real or imaginary worlds, rendered on a flat

	two-dimensional screen but appearing three-dimensional.
Virus	A malicious program, downloaded from a web site or disc, designed to wipe out information on your computer.
Volume	An area of storage on a hard disc. A volume is formatted by using a file system, such as FAT or NTFS, and has a drive letter assigned to it.
W3C	The World Wide Web Consortium that is steering standards development for the Web.
WAIS	Wide Area Information Server, a Net-wide system for looking up specific information in Internet databases.
WAN	A communications network connecting geographically separated computers, printers, and other devices.
WAV	Waveform Audio (.wav) - a common audio file format for DOS/Windows computers.
Web	A network of hypertext-based multimedia information servers. Browsers like Explorer are used to view any information on the Web.
Web Page	A document, usually HTML, that is accessible on the Web.
Web server	A computer that is maintained by a system administrator or Internet service provider (ISP) and that responds to requests from a user's browser.

Webmaster	One whose job it is to manage a web site.
WINSOCK	A Microsoft Windows file that provides the interface to TCP/IP services.
Wizard	A Microsoft tool that asks you questions and then creates an object depending on your answers.
WWW	See Web.
XML	Extensible Markup Language. A widely used system for defining data formats. XML provides a very rich system to define complex documents and data structures such as invoices, molecular data, news feeds, glossaries, inventory descriptions, real estate properties, etc.

Appendix A

Keyboard Shortcuts

The following keyboard actions are the standard shortcuts for working with Internet Explorer 6 and Outlook Express 6.

Keyboard Shortcuts for Explorer 6

Shortcut	Action
Shortcut	*Action*
Viewing Web Pages	
F1	Open Explorer Help
F11	Toggle fullscreen view
Tab	Move forward through object items
Sh+Tab	Move backward through object items
Alt+Home	Go to Home page
Alt+⇒	Go to the next page
Alt+⇐	Go to the previous page
Sh+F10	Display shortcut menu for link
F6	Move forward between frames
Sh+Ctrl+Tab	Move back between frames
⇑	Scroll up a document
⇓	Scroll down a document
PgUp	Large scroll up a document
PgDn	Large scroll down a document
Home	Move to the beginning of a document
End	Move to the end of a document
Ctrl+F	Find on this page
F5	Refresh Web page if necessary
Ctrl+F5	Refresh Web page if necessary or not
Esc	Stop downloading a page
Ctrl+O	Go to a new location
Ctrl+N	Open a new window
Ctrl+W	Close the current window

Shortcut	*Action*
Ctrl+S	Save the current page
Ctrl+P	Print the current page or active frame
Enter	Activate a selected link
Ctrl+E	Open Search in Explorer bar
Ctrl+I	Open Favorites in Explorer bar
Ctrl+H	Open History in Explorer bar
Ctrl+click	Open multiple folders (History/Favorites)

Using the Address bar

Alt+D	Select text in the Address bar
F4	Display Address bar history
Ctrl+ ⇐	Move cursor left to next '.' or '/'
Ctrl+ ⇒	Move cursor right to next '.' or '/'
Ctrl+Enter	Add 'www.' and '.com' to typed text
⇑	Move up AutoComplete list
⇓	Move down AutoComplete list

Working with Favorites

Ctrl+D	Add page to Favorites
Ctrl+B	Open Organize Favorites box
Alt+ ⇑	Move item up Favorites list
Alt+ ⇓	Move item down Favorites list

Editing

Ctrl+X	Cut to the Clipboard
Ctrl+C	Copy to the Clipboard
Ctrl+V	Insert Clipboard contents
Ctrl+A	Select all items on Web page

Using Print Preview

Alt+P	Set printing options and print the page
Alt+U	Change page settings
Alt+Home	Display first page to be printed
Alt+ ⇐	Display previous page to be printed
Alt+A	Type number of page to be displayed

Shortcut	*Action*
Alt+⇒	Display the next page to be printed
Alt+End	Display the last page to be printed
Alt+Minus (-)	Zoom out
Alt+Plus (+)	Zoom in
Alt+Z	Display a list of zoom percentages
Alt+F	Specify how to print frames
Alt+C	Close Print Preview

Keyboard Shortcuts for Outlook Express 6

Shortcut	*Action*
General	
F1	Open help topics
Ctrl+A	Select all messages
Main Mail Window	
Ctrl+O	Open the selected message
Ctrl+Q	Mark a message as read
Tab	Move between window panes
Main and Read Message Windows	
Ctrl+D	Delete a message
Ctrl+F	Forward a message
Ctrl+I	Go to your Inbox
Ctrl+M	Send and receive mail
Ctrl+N	Open a new message
Ctrl+P	Print the selected message
Ctrl+R	Reply to the message author
Sh+Ctrl+R	Reply to all
Ctrl+U	Go to next unread message
Ctrl+⇒	Go to next message in the list
Ctrl+⇐	Go to previous message in the list
Alt+Enter	View properties of selected message
Sh+Ctrl+B	Open Address Book
Ctrl+Y	Go to folder
New Message Window	
F3	Find text
F7	Check spelling
Esc	Close a message
Ctrl+K	Check names
Ctrl+Enter	Send a message
Sh+Ctrl+S	Add a signature
Alt+S	Send a message

Shortcut   *Action*

Main News Window

Sh+Ctrl+A	Mark all news messages as read
Ctrl+J	Go to next unread newsgroup
Sh+Ctrl+M	Download news for offline reading
Ctrl+O	Open the selected message
Ctrl+Q	Mark a message as read
Ctrl+W	Go to a newsgroup
Ctrl+Y	Go to a folder
Tab	Move between window panes
⇐ or +	Expand a news thread
⇒ or -	Collapse a news thread

Main and Read Message Windows

F5	Refresh headers and articles
Ctrl+F	Forward a message
Ctrl+G	Reply to all
Ctrl+N	Post new message to the newsgroup
Ctrl+P	Print the selected message
Ctrl+R	Reply to the author
Ctrl+⇒	Go to the next message in the list
Ctrl+⇐	Go to previous message in the list
Alt+Enter	View properties of selected message
Sh+Ctrl+U	Go to next unread conversation

New Message Window

Sh+Ctrl+F	Find text
Esc	Close a message
Ctrl+K	Check names
Alt+S	Send a message
F7	Check spelling

Appendix B

Internet File Formats

While downloading files from the Web, you will encounter many different types of electronic file formats. The way to identify a file's type is to look at its extension, typically shown as a dot followed by 2 to 4 letters (such as .jpg). You may need to identify the file type to know whether it will work on your computer, and whether you will need a particular type of software to decompress, play, or view it.

All of the file formats found on the Internet can be divided into one of two types: **ASCII** text files you can view with WordPad or Notepad, and **Binary** which contain non-ASCII characters and cannot be viewed.

We include here a guide to the most common Internet file formats with details of how some of them can be viewed, or played.

Plain Text (ASCII) Files

.html/.htm — The language in which Web documents are authored. Their file type is ASCII and they can be viewed in Notepad, but they require a Web browser like Internet Explorer to interpret their code and display the Web page correctly.

.txt — An ASCII text file which can be viewed with Notepad, or WordPad if they are very large.

Formatted Documents

.doc
Used for formatted ASCII text files, but also for documents created in some word processors, such as Microsoft Word and Windows versions of Wordperfect.

.pdf
Portable Document Format, a binary format developed by Adobe Systems Inc., that allows formatted documents to be transferred across the Internet so they look the same on any machine. Requires a Reader which is freely available directly from Adobe.

.ps
A PostScript file is unreadable except by a PostScript printer, or with an onscreen viewer like GhostScript.

.rtf
Microsoft Rich Text Format for text and graphics interchange that can be used with different output devices, operating environments, and operating systems. Most word processors are able to create, load, and read .rtf files.

Compressed and Encoded Files

.arc
An old binary format for archiving and compression, which can be manipulated by several programs, but especially ZipMagic.

.arj
A binary format for MS-DOS machines, especially in Europe. You can use WinZIP, or ZipMagic.

.bin
A Macbinary II Encoded File requiring Stuffit Expander.

.exe   A DOS or Windows binary executable program or self-extracting file. Launched by double-clicking on the file's icon.

.gz/gzip   The GNU Project's compression program, a binary format most commonly used for UNIX and PC files. Use ZipMagic which handles this format the same way as Zip files.

.hqx   A Macintosh binary file that has been converted into ASCII text so it can be safely transferred across the Net. Use BinHex13 (binhex13.zip) on a Windows PC to un-binhex it.

.sit   A Macintosh binary file that has been compressed using the Stuffit program. Use Stuffit Expander for Windows.

.sea   A Macintosh self-extracting binary archive file.

.tar/.tar.gz/.tar.Z/.tgz

These binary files are often found on Unix-based Internet sites. WinZip and ZipMagic handle all these formats the same way as Zip files.

.uu , .uue   UUencoded binary file. Used to convert binary data into text so it can be sent via e-mail. Explorer automatically decodes this type. You can also use WinCode to UUdecode files in Windows.

.Z   A UNIX binary compression format. Use WinZip or ZipMagic to decompress and view files with this extension.

.zip   A common binary compression standard for DOS and Windows that uses the DOS utility PKZIP. These files can be decompressed on the PC with WinZIP, or ZipMagic.

Graphics Files

.gif   One of the most common graphics file formats on the Internet, it stands for Graphics Interchange Format. Explorer views these automatically.

.jpg/jpeg   A popular binary compression standard used for photos and still images. Explorer also views these automatically.

.mng   Multiple-image Network Graphics (pronounced 'ming'), an image format like png that supports multiple images, animation and transparent JPEGs.

.png   Portable Network Graphics Format (pronounced 'ping'), is an extensible file format for faster images intended as a patent-free replacement for the GIF format. It uses lossless compression, so does not distort the image.

.tiff /.tif   A very large, high-resolution binary image format. You can use Lview Pro or PaintShopPro on a Windows PC.

Sound or Audio Files

.au/uLaw/MuLaw

Common sound formats (binary) found on the Web.

.aiff/.aif

A fairly common Macintosh sound format found on the Web.

.mid/ .rmi

Musical Instrument Digital Interface files.

.mp3

MPEG Audio Layer 3. Advanced compression technique for small near-CD-quality audio files. The most popular file format on the Web for distributing CD-quality music. A 1 MB file is equal to about one minute of music.

.ra/.rm/.ram

Real Audio, pioneering format for streaming audio on the Web optimised for low-to-medium speed connections.

.wav

Audio for Windows, the native sound format for Windows.

.wma

Windows Media file - the format used by the Windows Media Player to save compressed audio files to your hard disc.

Video and Multimedia Files

.asf

Advanced Streaming Format is Microsoft's streaming format. Can include audio, video, scripts, ActiveX controls, and HTML documents.

.avi

Audio Visual Interleave, a standard binary video format for Windows.

.mov/.qt/.qt3	Common binary formats for QuickTime movies, the Macintosh native movie platform.
.mpg/.mpeg	A standard binary format for 'movies' on the Internet, using the MPEG compression scheme. There is an MPEG FTP Site that has a large collection of MPEG player resources for all platforms (Mac, Windows, and UNIX).
.ra/.ram/.rm/.rmm	RealNetworks, RealAudio, and Real-Video files.
.rv	Real Video, format for streaming video on the Web optimised for low-to-medium speed connections.
.swf	ShockWave Flash from Macromedia for delivery of graphics and animation on the Internet.
.vdo	VDOLive file.
.viv	VivoActive Format for compression of streaming video, particularly over low bandwidth.
.vrml	Virtual Reality Modelling Language, is an open standard for the definition of 3-dimensional environments used on the Web.
.vob	DVD video format.

If you need any of the software mentioned, a search with Google.com should rapidly show you where to download it from.

A useful site with what must be a complete list of file extensions and their meanings can be found at:

www.webopedia.com/quick_ref/fileextensions.html

Windows Media Player

Most of the multimedia file types listed in this Appendix can be played by the Microsoft Windows Media Player, that was released with Windows 98 and updated with Windows XP. The listing below is taken from the Help system that came with the latter version.

Supported File Types

You can play the following types of digital media files with Windows Media Player. You can also select Windows Media Player as the default player for any of the listed file types.

File Type (Format)	File Name Extension
CD audio	.cda
Intel Indeo video technology	.ivf
Audio Interchange File Format (AIFF)	.aif, .aifc, and .aiff
Windows Media audio and video files	.asf, .asx, .wax, .wm, .wma, .wmd, .wmv, .wvx, .wmp, and .wmx
Windows audio and video files	.avi and .wav
Moving Picture Experts Group (MPEG)	.mpeg, .mpg, .m1v, .mp2, .mpa, .mpe, .mp2v, .mpv2
Musical Instrument Digital Interface (MIDI)	.mid, .midi, and .rmi
AU (UNIX)	.au and .snd
MP3	.mp3 and .m3u
DVD video	.vob

Index

Companion Discs

COMPANION DISCS are available for most computer books written by the same author(s) and published by BERNARD BABANI (publishing) LTD, as listed at the front of this book (except for those marked with an asterisk).

There is no Companion Disc for this book

To obtain companion discs for other books, fill in the order form below, or a copy of it, enclose a cheque (payable to **P.R.M. Oliver**) or a postal order, and send it to the address given below. **Make sure you fill in your name and address** and specify the book number and title in your order.

Book No.	Book Name	Unit Price	Total Price
BP		£3.50	
BP		£3.50	
BP		£3.50	
Name .... Address		Sub-total	£.............
		P & P (@ 45p/disc)	£.............
		Total Due	£.............
Send to: P.R.M. Oliver, West Trevarth House, West Trevarth Nr Redruth, Cornwall, TR16 5TJ			

PLEASE NOTE

The author(s) are fully responsible for providing this Companion Disc service. The publishers of this book accept no responsibility for the supply, quality, or magnetic contents of the disc, or in respect of any damage, or injury that might be suffered or caused by its use.